# <u>GENESIS</u>:

## A Social Vision.

*Forensic Essays on the Psyche, the World Mind,
and the Body Politic.*

# Troy Cochran

ISBN: 978-1493649112

*Also by the author:*
**Stone & Bone**
**The Gospel of Troy**

The author may be contacted at:
*delirioustill@gmail.com*
or
*trojanverses@blogspot.com*

# TABLE OF CONTENTS

## ACKNOWLEDGEMENTS

I do not find much useful information coming out of the universities or the television, so all credit for my education goes to the unsung heroes of the Great Awakening: to the clairvoyants and channels who have weathered all ridicule and condemnation from those of a more conventional learning to bring us a greater vista and clarity of understanding. Without the example of their integrity and daring, I would still be as muttonheaded as I was before I could read.

Insofar as the present work is concerned, my appreciation goes out to the late Jane Roberts and her boy Seth. The Seth Material has been the absolute bedrock foundation of my education and training. It puts all other textbooks to shame.

I'm grateful to the late Rudolf Steiner, in particular for his insights into the threefold social order -- source material for my seventh essay herein contained. Translations of his work can be found at the Rudolf Steiner Archives. (www.rsarchive.org.)

I have borrowed several terms from the Urantia Book, a massive work channelled in the mid-1930's -- terms for which we have no English equivalents. The Urantia Book, though some-times difficult to digest, is still an excellent source of material on philosophy and ethics, to name but two areas. It represents to me a training of the highest levels of university -- what a university education *should* be. The Urantia Foundation (www.urantia.org) is an excellent resource for those who are interested.

J.Z. Knight and her boy Ramtha have both impressed me mightily on a broad range of subjects. (See: www.ramtha.com.) And I should mention the work of Lee Caroll (www.kryon.com), Esther Hicks (www.abraham-hicks.com), and Darryl Anka (www. bashar.org), other channels who are of ongoing inspiration and delight to me. There are others that I could mention, but that will have to suffice.

In days to come, these are the kinds of people and the teachings that will stand head and shoulders above the rest; for though they win no laurels, and are seldom given credit for the influence they actually bring to bear on those who *do* win the laurels, they continue to provide for the world a royal service the likes of which there is no compare.

Thank you, thank you, thank you!

### Earth Prime.

*The bullfrog
makes a space around him
with his bulbous talk.
No one enters through the gate
without a password.*

*He sits upon his one
Gibraltar of a rock.
The Moon illuminates
all round
a whole platoon of monstrous
shapes,
pays them all in gold
doubloons,
but no one ever finds him out.*

*No shape was ever made
that matches, pound for pound,
his one hypnotic thought.
He sits
upon the whole world
as an Egg
that incubates
but never hatches.*

*Mosquitoes seek to take
the truth out with their long syringes;
but people nowadays
stay barricaded indoors
when black-clad crickets try to lure them out
into the portal
where the bullfrog's serenade
initiates the startled
trippers in the dark into the hole
of sound
where the world was started.*

FORWARD

## *Couriers From the Lettuce Sprouts and the Messengers of Lightning.*

Let's take a walk, you and I.

Imagine yourself strolling along with me on a fine summer day. The sun is in our eye at times, but the breeze is okay: it carries the evanescent brine of the Mediterranean and the pungent cooking of the region. This is some time ago, so we're sporting the latest togas from Athens and Rome. The dust of our travels, saffron and cinnamon, is getting in between our toes, because we have to wear these damn sandals wherever we go (sneakers have not been invented yet), but we pretend not to mind. In fact, we are too engrossed by the sight of a curious man sitting in a puddle of agitated people, just over there on the corner by the fish and vegetables. We hardly notice anything else.

These are a zealous and religious people, so the story goes, so they are evidently trying to teach the teacher. We don't either of us speak the native language around here, but it is easy to see that the teacher is not having any of it. He seems to be a fine fellow, though; he is listening patiently, a barely detectable smile working up to a mischievous grin.  The others are all talking at once.

I nudge you with an elbow.  "I know who that is," says I.  "That's that teacher they were telling us about last night at the inn, Yeshua ben ... what's-his-name.  And those must be some of his students."  (A mutual pause to consider the reasonableness of this, then:) "Don't look too agreeable, do they?"

"Not really.  What do you s'pose they're arguing about?" asks you.

I consider the question for a moment, but my mind was already made up.  "Well," says I after a good long spell, knowing how it annoys you when I act like I know what's really going on; but I'm paying the bills on this trip, so you look real interested.  "Well, they *are* Jews, after all; and you know how that lot can be.  What are Jews *always* going on about?  The kingdom to come!  The damnable Roman Empire!  The difficulty of getting out of bed in the morning!  The cost of bread!  Look at 'em:  they're worried about the economy!"

"In other words," says you, "no different than the rest of us."

"Exactly," says I.  "But that fellow in the center there, he's not having any of this, is he?  He's just waiting to get a word in edgewise, and then he's going to tell them all over again what he always talks about:  what's his gospel again?"

"The 'kingdom of heaven'," says you, remembering better than I the conversations of the night before.  (In my defense, I had to sleep on the floor:  didn't get a wink in.)

10

"Yeah, that's it, the 'kingdom of heaven.' Only, how do you talk to a relatively frightened, literal-minded people about an *invisible world,* when all they want is a *Revolution?*"

And now I've got to my main point, so here the vision fades as we take a last, long gaze at the curious blend of humor and consternation on the face of that intriguing young teacher.

I find myself in somewhat the same situation with my readers: one part of me is brimming over with revolutionary ideas about a new world: *the recolonization of America; cooperative economics; the sovereignty of the individual!* But another part of me is quietly working up to a mischievous grin, wondering about the mansion worlds and quantum particles: all the things we *can't* see, but that seem to be implied in the very fabric and tapestry of things.

The greatest challenge of a lifetime seems to be the gargantuan task of getting out of one's own way; or, put more intriguingly, of *extending the range of one's sensorium.*

As a typical human being, circumscribed by the habits of my imagination and perception (by the obvious and the redundant), I can easily sympathize with the notion of making the world a better place. And I have evolved a few spanking new ideas along that line, which I will be proudly showing off in the course of these essays. Yet, I also feel the frustrations of this inherently limited range of human purview as acutely as the next desperado for socio-political reform and a fatter wallet. Tomorrow, it seems, is less about reinventing government and economy, more about reinventing yesterday. As a sometime-philosopher, I wonder how things might look if I could get my head *above* the level of time and space -- to be on the outside looking in, so to speak. What is *before and after* the arrow of time? What is *within the closet* of a lump of space?

11

I feel the pull of some spiritual gravity that seeks to defy the normal agreed upon arrangement of things; a private religion almost, that has nothing to do with appeasing some tribal deity. There is something gigantic and momentous occurring even in a particle; a multiverse administration that oversees even our down-to-earth evolution. All our pet theories and policies, and even our best models of reality, are really rather laughable. The "Big Bang," for example: what was there to bang before anything was bangable? As Yeshua ben what's-his-name might have been about to tell his over-anxious students a moment ago, "What's the point of wasting effort on a kingdom of stone if you can't even distinguish between the 'kingdom' and the 'stone'? Nature apart from nature's Source is not even an episode: it's just a *reflection*. To change your face in a mirror, you don't wrestle with the mirror. You change your *expression!* Learn to develop your *perspective:* seek first the *Observer* of the surrounding invisible -- within *yourself* -- and everything else will stand out more brilliant and endearable."

So I have been doing something rather unorthodox and a little bit frightening: I have been learning how to listen to the couriers from the lettuce sprouts and the messengers of lightning.

That is, I have been learning to not take myself too seriously; yet not too lightly either. Win or lose, I will be the tortoise *and* the hare. So, yes, I have a few good ideas, and I intend to share them. And they may just end up as a scattering of seeds by the wayside, but you never know. In the meantime, I follow the pull of Source, trying to imagine what that may be; and the older I become the more interested I am in what I *cannot* see. The obvious and familiar has slight charm for me anymore: there is mold on the cheese, and even the aroma is a little dubious. Now I look to add new dimension to every little thing I see in my old landscapes, and mindscapes, and whatever comes in between.

My universe has become a beautiful woman of mystery. I cannot get my mind properly on anything else.

It makes for a great start, this having a body; but after awhile it gets annoying. Between now and the hour I set this tortoise mode of living completely aside, I will have to live with split loyalties. Yes, I must still eat and sleep and tend to bodily needs and noises, daily expenses, social relations with others of my kind similarly distressed; but I can also go exploring in other realms of thought than these daily redundancies. I can delve for new layers of *meaning* still more or less forbidden, and feel around for those more precious *feelings* than any of these semi-precious ones I can't even *give* away. Little by little, *I can alter the focus of my own perceiving.*

I am as logical as the next man, more or less, but for the life of me I cannot be objective *all* the time: my insides are sloshing around in sugared-up chemicals. I'm bonded together by too many frequencies. It's too noisy. It's too graffiti. But there are others who have gone out ahead of me; not all are dragging their knuckles up from behind. Some have already let go of all unnecessary struggles and gone far, far ahead of even their mortality. They are remembering me, and reaching back in thought to give a hand. They are talking to me quietly. They seem to understand why I cling so tenaciously to my unfinished ends, and that I have completions I am reaching for. They are helping me to be a bona fide dweller in the mansion worlds *already*, those premium places and those premium moments where curiosity *really* begins.

I have come to feel a little sorry for the religiously stoned and the scientifically specimened. Religionists often seem to miss out on a deeper spirituality, even though it's operating in their very bones. They think the "kingdom of heaven" is somewhere else. And the thoroughly optical often seem to miss out on certain moral heights altogether. They are just intellectual. Faith and reason, mumbling off on their own, or nibbling at each others' egos, is a sad, sad spectacle. There must be some unifying principle that goes largely unnoticed; that compensates a clergyman for being fundamentally illogical, and prevents cold arrogance from freezing to death on the summit of its own pinnacle.

To my way of thinking, we are not ever going to solidify the "truths" and "facts" of our chattering minds into self-evident Wisdom plain enough for *all* to see and wonder at, amazed. We are too two-dimensional, too polarized, in our approach to things, because we *try* though we cannot ever quantify and measure *all* invisible things; and we cannot completely reconcile that enormous gap between a naturally occurring *thing* and the *Source* of that occurrence. Ultimately, both "God" and "Energy" must be reckoned with if we are going to look honestly into the *intelligent design of things.* And I would be embarrassed to look at life in any other way. This is innately a religious *and* scientific quest for broader understanding. Anything less would be but half an orange. Not enough for a *real* appetite.

But there is a "divine paradox" here. We have only our time-and-space-bound minds with which to *reason* with; with which to reach out in *faith.*

Doesn't that just aggravate?

We need about equal parts *reason* and *faith* to bridge the gulf between what we know and do not know, and ultimately *cannot* know -- at least not on this side of the grave. We are innately saddled with the normal human difficulty of accepting realities not visible to us; yet also *driven* by an innate need to know: What is down those stairs in the darkness below? What is that creaking in the attic, where the wind ain't supposed to blow? Trouble is, we act as if our religious "truths" and scientific "facts" are Absolute. They are not, insofar as our foreshortened vision can see. They are just dusted off hypotheses, always falling off the mantlepiece. A *point of view* is always relative to the one doing to looking, the direction of his aim, and what he's standing on to give him his almighty altitude. Even a divine scripture still has to be *interpreted* to the satisfaction of a deciding mind.

But reason and faith are one-legged animals whenever they try to stand all by themselves. Even a wooden stool needs at least *three* legs to stand up on, and they're dumb as stumps. Which is to say: we must not let our grand and glorious Reason run away from our lovely Faith, or vice versa. Both mean well, they are just opposite sex. We must stand them before our most revered Intuition and get them hitched.

The bottom line is: we cling over-much to a rather narrow *sensorium*. We hang out in our daily mid-conscious minds, (if even that), and do not go too far below into the subconscious realms except to fall headlong into a cowardly sleep; nor up into the superconscious realms lest we seem to lift ourselves up in overestimation, above our stations. Yet, as we get past these terrible phobias about what's *really* "above" and "below" us; as we *broaden that sensorium,* through the continual exercise of our imaginations and reason and intuition -- a *three-legged* intelligence -- then we develop an open and active mind, as opposed to the buddy system of never thinking alone. This is the way to a greater psychological maturity: the way toward a lessening of fixation on familiarities, and the gradual transfer of identity and focus and priority from the world of mere quantities to the world of more *qualitative realities:* realities of greater intellectual *meaning* and spiritual *value.* That is, a "physical" reality of less density and greater *range.*

At the same time, education is a process, so we shouldn't *condemn* ourselves for our present fixations. Only if

15

you're sitting a full head taller than all the other students in the class, and sprouting whiskers, should there be any cause for alarm. (Particularly if you're female.) But it is not a crime to be human, any more than a preschooler is at fault for being something less than a graduate. But life *is* an evolutionary journey, and progression is expected, even of ourselves. Who wants to remain an idiot? But the dogma of "original sin" -- the idea that we are innately flawed, spiritually depraved, living under some kind of sentence -- is a great hindrance to our intellectual and spiritual maturity; as is the scientific attitude of narrow reasoning, clinging so exclusively to the five-senses world -- to the same sensorium we started out with in infancy -- afraid to wander experientially, even *intellectually*, into a six-senses world, or an eight-senses world; or even (God forbid!) a thirty-senses world -- nearly *seven* times as big!

I like the word *sensorium*, you may have guessed. I like the idea of putting a name upon our sensory and conceptual capabilities, at the same time implying that that range can be *broadened* -- in terms of both *per*ception and *con*ception; that there are subtle circuitries of "mind" and "spirit" just as there are obvious circuitries of the body once we look beneath the skin and muscle; or deeper still, into the subtle, yet still quantifiable, circuitries of the cellular levels. But then this begs the question of what is "body," when we start delving into the molecular matrix and atomic orbits; then the circuitries become extremely difficult to quantify; still more so in the subatomic realms -- systems of heat transfer through electron and other quantum dynamics, that *also* convey "information" (... no one wants to use the word "consciousness" or "mind" at this point).

But I cannot for the life of me find any actual dividing line between "mind" and "body"; presumably there is none between mind and "spirit" either; so that we must ultimately wonder what we *really* mean by these terms, and what constitutes the *reality* of their differentials. Are there differing circuits and strata of

16

mind, as there are of body?  Are there differing circuits and strata of spirit?  Are we active and communicable at *super*-conscious levels as we are at *sub*-conscious and *mid*-conscious levels?  Are we not just creating conceptual and perceptual limitations where no walls actually exist?  Are we not just afraid of a different kind of "dark"?

So, ultimately, our religion cannot get out ahead of our science, and our science cannot really get out ahead of our religion.  They are Siamese twins:  they see the same girl, but see her differently; yet they cannot either of them woo her separately without upsetting the other one.  Now, if they put their heads *together* for a change, it would be a more interesting party.

And who is this pretty girl in my homely analogy?

Why, she is that terrible allurement of feminine *intuition*. She is something of a gypsy, who knows more than she ought to, and respectable elders have no idea what to do with her.  It is a bit confusing, because while we have evolved long-standing institutions of faith and logic, we are slower to worship at the altars of intuition.  We are creatures of *electrochemistry*, and that is a loud cacophony of noises to be getting along with. What with all those hormones and neuropeptides screaming up and down the streets of the brain and bloody arteries, it is without question a lived-in neighborhood.  It is a wonder anyone can hear the birds chirping, squirrels cheeching, the ocean of the wind wafting, let alone some hypothetical gaggle of midwayers and angels  watching and teaching.

It does not seem to me that the Grand Creation came about impossibly, or was ever left alone to evolve itself, in part and in whole, haphazardly.  I think there is an overcontrol of evolution just too difficult for us to see, being tadpoles yet in the murky pond of our local Being.

17

But we are still a work in progress. In due time, I trust, we will have our institutions of intuitional practice, our psi corps academies of this discipline and that, just as we have had, and still have, our temples to logic and faith. We are like the God of our long imaginings, but in his Trinity, or Chaos in its trigonometric equilibrium of opposite charges: we also are triune in nature -- body, mind, spirit; or *electrochemistry, pattern,* and *potential* -- and the successful achievement of our preferments is as much a process of trinitization as anything. The great "I AM" that is both Unity and Trinity -- three in one, and one in three -- is mirrored in every particle. It is the ladder, or the spiral staircase, by which we both ascend and descend -- like Jacob's dream-ladder -- only it's our DNA we're climbing about in.

Or we can extend the picture out to God the Sevenfold, reflected in the septet organization of physical reality -- in the seven colors of the rainbow, the basic frequencies of visible light, of the musical scale, of the electron clouds enshrouding every atom. It is as impossible to escape the Law of Seven as it is the Law of Three, or the Law of One.

Again, there is no getting out of the way of "God" and "Energy." The Unity, the Threefold, the Sevenfold, and the Manifold basis of all strata of Reality ultimately cannot be avoided; cannot be short-circuited. It *is* the encircuited. We work from this glue always. And there is no way around, but *through* it.

We are thus limited not only by our creature conditions, but by our prejudices along the way. In the essays that follow, I will be probing into themes primarily religious and scientific -- *intuitively* led, or so I aim. I am tripply yoked to a team of three mighty and stubborn oxen: God-as-Source, God-as-Judge, and God-as-Nonexistence. I am sure to be dragged all over the field, and into the neighbor's corn, but so be it.

And in such enterprises as philosophy -- no different than any other field of endeavor, really -- one can only explore through *metaphors*, in lieu of Absolutes, which lie a tad beyond our little reach. Ultimately, we only *pretend* to arrive at understandings that are really only attainable at transcendent levels -- beyond verbal comprehension and image-bound understanding. But that's good enough for me, where's the beach?

And if even I cannot trust my metaphors to guide me always, I hope you are wise to abandon them at some point also. It's good to walk in another man's shoes, but never for too long, or your "under-standings" will come to smell just as badly as his.

We are just passing through these parts, never making a home for good. Home is what we bring with us, neglected in a pocket. It is rather like using the old British coin system of pounds, shillings, and pence to arrive at a sum of Absolute and fabulous wealth. But stretch all our mighty earnings howsoever we will, one gold sovereign, seven shillings, and a thre'pence barely amounts to a pocketful of change. In the same way, for all our noble efforts and exemplary methods, God the Sovereign, God the Threefold, God the Sevenfold, and God the Manifold, still seem to leave me sitting on a rather flattened wallet.

\* \* \*

I have spent over thirty years exploring and maturing the ideas and ideals of my beloved social vision. It has become an old whisky aged in charred barrels of oak and hickory. To drink it straight from a tin can will burn a hole in your shorts, and rob you of your stomach lining. But one cannot make his mark in the world without leaving some kind of stain. I apologize in advance for any discomfort this may cause you.

A vision of the future is advanced by postulates; and I have gone out as far as a man *can* go, postulating (in a playful manner) a futuristic point of view, at an undisclosed time, after the slow decay and collapse of civilization as we know it -- its economic, political and judicial systems, education and religion, technological and industrial situations, etc. -- but not so far out that we of today, with our more basic and bug-infested systems, cannot more or less relate. I refer to that hypothetical future time as "Earth Prime," the idea being that the rather dysfunctional or primary systems of today are *there* marginalized, almost as secondary and substandard realities. I will be quoting and otherwise making reference to a purely fictional book, a future history of post-EuroAmerican times, called the *"**A**stronautical **S**ummary of the **T**ripartisan **A**rena of **R**eflective **I**nterplanetary Circuits of Association;"* or, in abbreviation, the *"Astari Circuits of Association;"* or simply the Astari Manuscript. As the Earth looks very calm and blue from the astronomical height of the moon, so does any given afternoon look from the astronomical height of near honesty.

The purpose of this outlandish approach is to create a clear contrasting scenario between what *is* and what *can be*, without being overly critical of today, or overly serious about tomorrow. It is not my intention to sound some clarion call to arms, to initiate a third-party or grassroots movement. I am well aware of the futility of trying to get the motivation up to fight another man's revolution; of the spiritual inertia that holds us to our designated posts in the land of apathy. In the long haul of time my work may inspire certain groups in certain barns and alleyways to create actual working models based on the blueprints herein, but that little concerns me at this point. Theoretical work necessarily foreshadows any practical application, and I have never been a very practical fellow. I am more concerned with helping a fellow laborer over the ditch than with the actual digging of it. The greater value of my social vision is simply in providing a theoretical mirror in which to better illuminate the features of the present age.

Cheers!

August 23, 2012
Eugene, Oregon

*"Let come what may in terms of political unrest:*
*Even troubled waters level*
*To their common best."*

**Cantos from the Ghost of Lincoln.**

*"Shortly after the restoration of the Interplanetary Circuits of Association, more commonly referred to as "the Shift" by the native peoples of the detention worlds, the global community of post-EuroAmerican cultures on Number 606 rebounded from the traumas of social disintegration with surprising agility and speed. While the mantle of economic power passed largely to the emerging industrial nations of its Africanus continent and the so-called Eastern "Orientus", in the tripartisan arena of recolonial politics stirring again in the dormancy of the troubled Americas and much of Europa a new spirit of enterprise ignited the imaginations of the decimated population: a spirit of enterprise no longer motivated exclusively by the profit motive of predatory industry, survivalism, and associations for mutual aid, but by a spirit far more radical. For the first time in the history of **any** of the quarantined worlds, individuals responded to the awakening circuits by coming together for the succor of those **outside** the clans. Thus was the Age of the Steward born, on the very sphere most disrupted by the severing of the constellation circuits."*

Astari Manuscript, Book II,
*The Enigma of Reflectivity.*

\* \* \* \* \* \* \*

## Essay 1:

## **Learning To Walk the Garden of Oblivion.**

"New Worlds" are always preceded by the well-meaning ineptitude of colonies.  Tyrants sooner or later give way to limited democracies.  And state sovereignty eventually gets traced back to its source in individual consent.  Thus, it is not all that difficult to project where the trends of history are taking us.  There will be new colonies, and new governments, and new ideas of citizenship and sovereignty.  Everything we hold sacred today will pass away; are already passing.  We are just clinging to anything that floats.  One thing is certain:  we are swimming in an ocean of debts -- as individuals, as corporations, as nations.  We are up to our throats.  We are down to our depths.  We are praying to the clouds, and shaking nervous with every passing squid and tuna fish: we cannot quite get the feel of what's moving underneath us. All in all, we are not very confident of living in a responsive universe.

It's not that we are shipwrecked. It's that we are fundamentally *spiritual.* We just don't know the difference.

We seem to think, overall, that growing up is some kind of punishment. One minute we were at the controls, feeling nautical; the next, we were amniotic! Our world became a womb, and our Father became a testicle. We have had to acclimate to brutal conditions; and that has made us, for all our miserable efforting, brutal. The so-called "soul," or everything that is most precious to us, is still embryonic. We mess about as best we can to get our situation straightened out; but let's be honest: we are mostly bobbing up and down like bait, wondering how we got here, and who's responsible. That it might have been our own free choice is something that we have not yet had long enough to rationally consider. Which brings us to the current age: the Age of Getting Over Our Insecurities and Looking After Each Other.

Something in the current era is different. A kind of "quiet revolution" has begun. I don't know what started it all; I must have missed something. I get the sense that the guns have gone out ahead of me, and I am left standing stupidly with the ammunition; which is to say, that a radical transformation has begun, unbeknownst to many people yet, evidently, so I have taken it upon myself to be its tag-along trumpeter.

It may be true that our government has long been subverted from its original design and purpose, point our fingers where we will; and that our daily repetitions and commercial habits are predicated upon a predatory economics. It little matters, really. In the final analysis, we make our own realities. It is a gradual process. It took humanity a long, long time to learn a limited form of democracy; it will take a while longer before we are ready to remove the restraints. It is not less true, despite our tendency to move at the speed of a glacier, that we are still pioneers on the cutting edge of a different kind of frontier, pushing our fears before it. We are still enamored of our technology. One day, we will be enamored of our spirit.

To say that *"we make our own realities"* is a bold affront to our courage, or lack of same; especially in our more entrenched citadels of faith and logic: in our sciences with their God of Chance, and in our religions with their God of War. I may be overstating things a mite, but don't stop me here I'm on a roll. To assume a sacred, creational stance as a truly sovereign *individual*, in the face of all that Black Robes and White Robes alike have long held holy, is indeed a revolutionary idea. The implications of this, as the notion grows more rampant in society; as more and more people come to question the very Authority of those who have presumed the right to define another's belief, another's duty; the implications for government, for law and order; for commerce and industry, as a dumb, defeated and subdued workforce wakes up from its long lethargy and decides to stretch its legs, its forgotten muscles, it very soul; the implications are staggering … impressive … unfathomable.

It will change everything.

It is being called the "Great Awakening," for it presumes a widespread slumber to the sum of millions, to the sum of billions -- humanity as a kind of sleeping giant, or a sprawling anthill of Lilliputians: a people so convinced of their littleness, their insignificance, under the bootheel of God or Government, Corporation, what have you, that for all intensive purposes we might as well be asleep. But here and there one stirs fitfully, would kick off the suffocating blankets; and everywhere is a general discontent, from long abuse and neglect -- a long-

27

suffering, well-indoctrinated *self*-neglect more than anything else. We are uncertain of our addictions: we fear it may be our faith … maybe our very emotions. We have so many sacred cows we do not name.

With all the standard rhetoric of reform still bandied about, which never really comes to any legitimate fruition; "jobs, change, a new economy," the old recipe; the occasional "tea party" reactions that beat their fists on the wall, have their little day, and fizzle out, accomplishing nothing; whispers of black helicopters equipped with mind-altering psychotronics, concentration camps that yet stand empty, cattle cars designed to transport human beings, and the like -- stories that hint of some nefarious orchestration of reality into which the drugged and befuddled masses are being steered; stories that, of course, cannot be substantiated. All of these new worries, intermixed with the same old public disgruntlement, evinces a pervasive spiritual malaise that no one wants to talk about. We go about our chores and entertainments, wanting answers, trying not to look amazed.

Who will save us from ourselves? Who will give our labor purpose and meaning? Who will make these night fears go away?

We are so in need of something new to think about.

But then there are the real changes: oddities in the environment; changing climates and weather patterns; subtleties in the new ones being born, already so much older than we; that new and peculiar form of individualized spirituality beginning to upset everything. What are the present and future implications of these?

There can be no doubt that we have been sold a rotten bill of goods. It doesn't matter who did the selling: we bought it.

28

We buy it still, every day, with our very lives.  It lies so far back in time anyway (if you want to get down to root causes), there is really nothing for it but to roll up our sleeves, sift through the debris of our lives, the debris of our *minds; ferret* out the lies; give up our dependencies on false aids;  tidy up our old debates, and come to new conclusions; set new preferences; set in motion the wheels of a new vision.   There is a need for enlightened preparation for the coming changes; for who can doubt that a critical juncture is fast coming upon us, when some things outlived their usefulness must pass away, and new ideas will want to be framed up against a doubting hesitation, like a newborn babe in the arms of one not yet grown accustomed. Sooner or later we'll want to put a name on this new potential pushing up in us for recognition.  It will take honesty, and all our resources.  It will take a broad tolerance in allowing the full array of all perspectives, old *and* new; for in the worlds to come, if we are to let go of old defeats and old defenses, at long last daring to assert individuality against a greedy and seductive oppression, every poor, put-upon little citizen must have a say, or someone else will speak up something different.  The wheels of some nebulous and nefarious Ambition are already rolling; we must ask ourselves a question:  What is it that so plagues us in our heart of hearts, that we lay down like dogs before those who are not master, to beg a bone from an unresponsive system that would have us be so submissive ... when we ourselves are the progenitors of all wealth, and the delegators of all secondary impositions?

In simpler terms:  What makes us so afraid to tweak a change?

*It is that our fundamental difficulties are not really political or economic*, regardless of the obvious manipulations in the pricing of certain commodities (gasoline comes easily to mind).   We allow certain criminalities to go relatively undisturbed, for now, (the pharmaceutical industry is *rife* with them), because we are plagued by deeper worries. As these are resolved, we naturally clean up our cultural environments. When we are not at war with ourselves, it is as easy to recycle a politician as an aluminum can. Self-government always comes down to what we really think of ourselves.

Underneath all our worries, we have evolved a profound and debilitating *distrust* of human nature; and this profound self-distrust undermines our social confidence at every turn. We fear to allow ourselves, as individuals, too much freedom or too much power -- we have a belief in, and fear of, "too much" -- and thus all too easily acquiesce to the most invasive regulations, because we have been cowed by the long overbearance of religion, and more recently by the arrogance of science: there are root assumptions in these mindsets that have for too long gone unquestioned -- that we are "sinners;" that there is something intrinsically wrong with us that justifies our being penned and put to harness, to "earn" the living we evidently do not deserve, and we are the first to agree; or that life is innately meaningless, a random occurrence, and human beings are "soulless," sourceless, scum on a pond -- the intellectual inferiors of the spiritually depraved. And in our absence, in our abdication, the way is paved for those of the greatest ambitions to assert themselves over the general good and basic needs of all others, to serve their own ends, whatever the cost to the public good. They position themselves to set the fees even upon the very basic necessities for *existence!* We pay them, without so much as a whimper for economic guarantees, as if we had no right to our own necessities. We give these predators the very tools they leverage against us. We do not even stand amazed.

We are dumbfounded.

But there is more to human nature than any particular mask we wear, however beautiful, however hideous. If there are those who operate in the dark, more or less, who choose to live

30

by stealth for shame of what they have done to themselves, and for what they are about to do; there are also those who more or less rise above all this cacophony of noise we make; who ally themselves, not to the hungers of the void in their chests (as we have all been too adroitly trained to do -- the symptoms of an embryonic soul starved of fulfillments), but rather by some fuller Presence of being seeking its own emergence up through all the layers of our sense and nonsense, character overladen to make its contribution when that moment comes for its one ripe season.

It is not a question anymore of neatly dividing "good" and "evil." Human nature, like its counterparts in all the other kingdoms, is too full of color, much too much to go long ignored, or too long contained. We must search and find out who we are, for we are not now who we used to be, and not yet what we aim to be. The boundaries between true "citizenship" and "criminality" have become obscured. The balance between "liberty" and "culpability" tips now this way and now that way, and we have lost our bearings; we no longer know where we stand, where we are: we have too many laws; we have not enough laws; now taxing, now spending; now needy, now greedy; now Christian, now Caesar; we dream of going back to old principles, to our Founding Fathers, but we are constrained by too many and too varied domain of changing circumstances: we must go forward.

Our enemies are invisible now; our friends have been too long ignored. What am I saying? We have only ever been our *own* invisible enemy, our *own* forgotten friend. We sweep too much under the rug of our national insecurity, for fear that we are bugs. But I think those quiet revolutionaries are right: we make our own realities ... whether by design or by default. We would choose better and wiser if we took more time to sift through all the tangle of our adolescent thoughts.

31

Christian, Muslim, Jew, elated, shattered:  Have we not still the selfsame children yet to feed and raise up right and mighty as we ourselves once stood?  Then we have promises to keep.  Let us get about them.

I say it with some chagrin, that we are rightly prideful, yet sensibly ashamed, of this so-called *federal* system we entertain.  It is in part a federation of states, but much of that is just pretend; by and large, we have consented to become an ugly oligarchy:  most of the power is shared between contending groups we never intended, who are given no mandate.  And what are these words anyway:  "federal," "national," "republican," "democratic":  I get the sense that no one remembers what we started out talking about way back when.  We got distracted into something else.

One day, I suppose, some cabal of fools will burn our Capitol to the ground.  That is okay, so long as we keep our own head and shoulders, our own bicameral brain.  We will manage.  In some nebulous way, we are our own legislators, our own presidents and chief justices -- or own *sovereigns* of heart and head, skilled hands and feet of clay -- all this officialdom we delegate and tolerate as best we can, these semi-representatives, is just so much play and mayhem.  In the grand view of things, it is all too devious to be taken too serious.  We are all of us masters of pretend.

Do you think it has all been in vain, this long evolution from Roman chains to Medieval peasantry to modern suffrage even before the legal drinking age?  We are meant to *become* what we are aiming for, we have not *arrived* at anything significant yet.  This that we are living now is only staging.  There are purposes we have only begun to glimpse, and no doubt many others beyond our guess.  Democracy must also, in its turn, give way to a greater refinement of authority, as all the monarchies and tyrannies before it; for democracy is *also* tyranny, when ignorance is syndicate. And government by *any* name is only temporary. When its purpose is served, it is dismantled and put away. It never was the purpose of government simply to govern, or to provide order and structure and limitation for no other reason than that is what a godly power does; and was *certainly* never the purpose of government to serve the whims of a few. That has only ever been the opinion of those few. Government is a trust, and there is always a reciprocal relationship between the governed and those given that trust. The purpose of that trust is to legislate, adjudicate, and execute *for* the people, *by* the people, what the people themselves very well know they would generally desecrate, if left to their own devices. "Government" is the request of the people for discipline against the very liberty they so extravagantly waste.

The people are *gods*, and deep down we all know this. But we are only at the larval stage. The doctrine of "original sin" has been our insurance against premature wisdom -- learning what is not of our earning -- and government has only ever been a back-up plan. The idea is that by accepting the imposition of *outward* controls, we would gradually learn the *inward* controls. Government, ideally, is the trustee of what we have been striving for, afraid to take hold. That is, we *delegate* our power away because of what it *Is*.

I started this essay with some rather vague and general comments about a "quiet revolution;" about a "spiritual malaise," and the slow emergence of a new train of thought and a growing momentum: a nation showing signs of waking up from a low, dispirited state of lethargy and grumbling agitation; a nation in many ways dissatisfied with prevailing conditions, yet still complacent. I am being purposely vague in my descriptions because we are dealing here with rather deep issues, and deep resistance -- more of a spiritual nature than a political or economic one, yet one which is bound to show effects in the domains of politics and economics sooner or later. As more and more people wrestle with their understandings over this dilemma of personal empowerment and the smearing or obliteration of the core of their identities -- Are we sovereign entities? Can we truly broaden our effect on reality? Ought we to trust ourselves further than we have yet dared? -- as this dilemma reaches its point of crisis and resolve, as surely it must, it heralds the beginning of a new era:  for it will bring to the foreground of public debate profound new questions revolving around the balance of sovereignty between the individual and the state.  It is one thing when the "consent of the governed" results in a dubious and nebulous and regulatory government, a predatory marketry, and a subdued workforce.  But how does one manage a people *aware* of their sovereignty, organized and expert, in civil and corporate and cultural deviance?  A people who dare to take "self-determination" to its next limit?

What happens to the Rule of Law when private *will* is sovereign?

What happens to "culpability" when sovereignty implies *full* self-responsibility (responsibility for *all* that one experiences)?  How then does one define "negligence" and "victimization" between *co-creators?*

What happens in the world of medicine when those responsible for their own diseases become responsible as well for their own healings?  What happens to the greedy conglomeration of pharmaceuticals and all their mechanizations?  What happens to insurance when the dogma of pending disaster goes out the window?

What happens to education when even teenagers, fed up with the impotence of parents and teachers, the constant invalidation of *their* intelligence, the tyranny of a federal curriculum, finally gather the courage to walk out of their institutions, to take charge of their *own* potentiality?

What happens to science and technology when *consciousness* is energy, and can no longer be smugly denied? What happens to psychology and psychiatry in the bright light of a self-proclaiming psyche that can no longer be lied to, breaking out of the cage of its superficiality?

What happens to corporate America when a Constitution guarantees the basic necessities of life to *every* citizen?

What happens to a congregation when a "sinner" stands up to the Monolith of Fear, and will make no more sacrifices for some ancient Hebrew disobedience?

Such questions as these ought to give some kind of indication that society is about to undergo a fundamental change. The "Shift" is upon us, and perhaps in a generation or so we will have become something entirely Else.

It little matters to a *sovereign* entity what the politicians are forever getting up to, or what the preachers are preaching, theorists are theorizing, judges are judging, inventors inventing, investors investing; nor even what the neighbors might be thinking. The government, the economy, the culture stutters forward in its old redundancies; nothing is new; nothing inspires; all are liars. People go about their days as they always do. Why should a sovereign entity be disturbed by any of this? They make their own realities. They exist with one foot in the mass-shared world of little follies, the other foot in another world most people yet know nothing about. The law, the social mores and fears, all manner of absurdities flow around them; for that which science ignores and religion forbids -- *the substantive nature of consciousness itself* -- is for this growing citizenry a creative medium. What engages their attention is not the dog-and-pony shows of the headline news, the latest nonsense out of Washington, the superstitions and inconveniences of homeland insecurity. Sovereignty is acquired little by little, in the gradual turning of the mind *away* from things not wanted, the infusion of concentrated attention toward something worthy: it is the art of *intentionally* collapsing the wave-function of probabilities into particle reality, what otherwise is done haphazardly. It is learning to walk the garden of oblivion. It is what we are *all* trying to do: to give up a life of redundancy for a life of meaning; to make some little private dream come true.

But we work against a tide of ignorance, squabbling over resources. We are divided in our loyalties: to one side, all that has outlived its usefulness, but yet commands our senses, our obligations, scatters our attention, dilutes us into a quivering mass of spineless jellyfish. To the other side, a barely imagined power and freedom: a vision of things to come, still congealing.

We can imagine all manner of dire things, if we are sloppy in our thinking ... and we are permeated with sloppy thinking: a slop, however, that is a mix of themes old and new. It is difficult for me to speak precisely about these themes, there are so many hidden variables. We are shaped by the convolutions of our beliefs, and they are manifold and tentacled. But I foresee that this "slop" will spill over into the public debates over all our superficial handling of vital issues -- health care, education, tax reforms and what not. It will slop over into cases before the courts of appeals, the pulpit, the classroom, the boardroom, the bedroom; it will slop over into the arts, become the stuff of poetry and novels and newspapers and television; it will become the stuff of mind-blowing technologies and new industries; it will wreak havoc with the superficialities of our worship. The rising sovereignty of the individual, and That from whence it comes, will seek its balance in the allocation of power and privilege to the state ... and the legal, corporate, economic, and cultural ramifications of this will be profound.

—

*"Rest in the certainty that you are not entirely alone,*
*All evidence to the contrary;*
*That, taken altogether, isolated dreamers make*
*A dreadful, silent Army."*

**Cantos from the Ghost of Lincoln.**

*"Without the natural endowment of the fiduciary powers in the minds of ascendent humans, there would have been no Morontia Temple, no Psi Corps, no Tripartisan Arena, and no Earth Prime. Indeed, there would have been no ascendent evolution! The physics of time would be entirely irrelevant without this fundamental response of the universal mind itself in suprafine discrimination, even in the innate logic, moral headings, and worshipfulness of the primitive mind. It is chiefly because of these three subliminal intuitions, in the hands of the indwelling Fiduciary in the upper strata of the mind of man, that the mid-mind functions of awakened humanity received that ultimatonic jolt it did, making the Shift possible in the 'nick of time,' so to speak. Only then were those secondary and tertiary events able to be orchestrated that so expertly opened the time locks and made possible the gradual welcoming of a unified Earth Prime into its rightful place in the Association of Worlds."*

Astari Manuscript, Book IV,
*Fundamentals of Psychometry.*

\* \* \* \* \* \* \*

Essay 2:

# A Provisional Framework for the Gropers in the Darkness of Tomorrow.

There is a spiritual current that runs through every age. Some are attuned to it, some are not. All are couched in its gaze. In our day, the leading thought is scoffed at and brushed away as just so much "New Age" mumbo-jumbo, airy-fairy nonsense. Most folk are doing all they can, in a culture of overwhelm, just to hurl themselves through a day, snarling over some bone or other, won't be bothered: they keep their eyes glued to their plates. In the language of another time: "Mankind are more disposed to suffer, while evils are sufferable, than to right themselves by abolishing the forms to which they are accustomed." This from the *Declaration of Independence.*

41

I'm well aware that much of what I have to say in offering the following ideas toward the creation of a provisional framework will fall on deaf ears. That is okay. I write to one part of every million. Here and there an agitated heart looks up from its dinner plate and weighs the needs of billions; would make the start of a startling contribution; is dripping with knowledge and talent; goes largely unrecognized as a social misfit, an oddity; an angel or a deviant, hard to say; a mind for clouds: a holistic healer; an independent; a steward of flowers. Here and there a group forms, searching out alternative ways, barely knit together; call them pioneers, or gropers in the darkness of tomorrow. These essays are written for them, the inhabiters of those rarest of proud towers, who have the lay of the land, and their eye on knowing more or less what to do.

Yes, that would be you.

For starters, let's roll out a big piece of paper, draw out a map of the virgin world, and label it: The Recolonization of Everything That's Already Been Started.

Next, let's have a simple threefold policy to keep us more or less on course. We'll call it: "The Three R's of a Global Education." Simply put, we will concern ourselves with:

1) The *Recolonization* of our communities;
2) The *Reclamation* of forgotten rights; and,
3) The *Reconstruction* of broken things toward new enterprise.

Now we have our map; some simple policies to guide us on our way; and a wide variety of hardy pioneers, new world dreamers, and social bushwackers scattered here and there. We need yet a "holding company" of sorts, to pull us all together in these new Plymouths and Virginias and Hudson Bays. Let's

42

keep it simple and sweet, and very general: may I refer to us as *public stewards?*

One more thing remains: a set of principles. How do we articulate those higher standards we already live by, the assertion of a unified Will that takes us beyond those dog-eared primary books we mastered under the Rule of Law? We'll not set sail until we put our signatures to a contract or a set of Articles: let's call them simply *The Codicils.*

Now to get some wind in our sails, and we'll be on our way.

I.

It does not take unthinkable amounts of investment capital and properties in a far off land to establish a colony. Wherever we make our meals and beds will do. A few friends with a shared vision, an ad hoc plan, some chinks in our pockets: *seeds in the hand!*

The driving force of a revolution only needs the momentum of an *idea*: and a powerful colony need be no more than just such a revolutionary idea, initially. Imagine something long enough, and it will come to be.

A colony is made strong, not by its material resources; these may be very meagre initially; it is made strong by its motivation, and held together by the purity of its cooperation. Initially, there is nearly always a tangle of individual motives, like weeds in a garden all wanting the same attention, and these will need to be sorted out periodically. Individual needs -- physical, financial, emotional -- have to be met, but stewardship does not restrict itself to the ideal of mutual aid: this implies a void at the center, and a membership essentially feeding upon one another.

43

A colony of public stewards, by its very definition, exists to serve the broader needs of those *outside* the group, as its prime directive. That automatically serves the needs of those within the group.

This gives us our first codicil, our Prime Directive: *to guarantee the basic needs of all outlying people, within the means of each respective colony, not neglecting the continual replenishment of its reserves.*

For now, let us save ourselves a world of trouble and go around the hornet's nest of human complaints and miseries: we know well enough what constitutes the "basic needs" of individuals -- what personal liberties and economic necessities, what free range of enterprise and opportunities -- but we do not want to lose our heads to all the slights and stings of some universal pity. We need only look to the ongoing failures of capitalistic and socialistic schemes alike to remind ourselves that governments and corporations cannot by themselves secure the fundamental guarantees so indispensable to their people. They rather prey upon the gullibility of the honest and simple, using every trick of privilege and secrecy. What forms of colonial government and management can best invoke the sovereignty of individuals, in responsible and sensible stewardship one to another ... well, that is the question of the day. That is innately the burden and the privilege of every colonial initiative. Toward that end, I have a few remarks to say.

In creating a provisional framework for a given colony, there is room enough to make a thousand blunders; but also opportunity for a thousand novelties. If governments essentially derive their powers (just *and* unjust) from the wise or placid consent of the governed (and bear in mind that governments are not only civil in nature, but corporate and religious also, to name but two), then the success of any provisional framework rests upon the question of *rightly invoking the sovereignty of those so engaged.* In other words, we have arrived upon that threshold of evolution in which humanity is poised to extend the political and social experiment from a *limited* to a more *direct democracy!* Needless to say, the implications of this are forbidding.

Let us lay to it anyway.

## II.

So that it be made plain, the question now before us is this: Can a people so govern themselves, assuming upon them-selves the greater share of mutual and self-responsibilities, so as to lessen the public reliance upon a sitting government, with its incumbent abuses?

There can be no doubt that representative democracy leaves itself as open to the abuses of rank and privilege as all the forms of government that have gone before it; and that, in the other direction, a self-actuating people would be just as prone to all the inroads of greed and manipulation. So long as human beings are riddled with insecurities, and their attendant frustrations, animosities, and desperations, goading ambition to circumvent propriety, so long will we have to contend with these chronic problems that plague our immaturity. But don't you see, that is the entire issue: it is fundamentally about, not some intrinsic flaw in human nature for which a sovereign Authority must be invoked to control and discipline -- that condemnation of *ourselves* is what agitates our insecurities, and gets up in us all manner of phobias and deviances. Rather, it comes down to simple issues of maturity. All the crimes and wars of humankind are reducible to runaway night-fears fostered in a primary nursery. We have not yet grown into our full estate and spiritual inheritance. That is it, and there never was just cause for the Puritan rod or the pulpit of shame. Our laws and social mores have too long been infected with this crying-out-loud for protections over some imagined boogeyman or social disease. And whilst we cling to the skirts of Mamma Church and Nanny Government, Big Money sneaks in and thieves.

For the life of me, I cannot imagine how a nation of wee toddlers and adolescents can manage themselves without recourse to some damned congress or parliament or papacy. But we are not *all* toddlers and adolescents, now are we? If we can rise to the call of environmental stewardship in the face of a global warming, then we can surely rise to the necessity for stewardship across the board. Who are the stewards of our industry and economy? Who are the stewards of technology? Who are the stewards of culture and education, of our dilapidating cities with their refuse and homeless and traffic and machinery? Who are the stewards of our homeland security? If it is not we ourselves, then it is some bureaucratic oligarchy, and we are a republic in name only.

There is but one legitimate government, and it is not a "mediocracy." It is a conscience.

If there is no nation of individuals who can yet govern themselves directly, without recourse to all the chicanery of mis-representation; if "sovereignty" is still so frightening that it must be denied or delegated away to any open mouth that gobs it; then I can see but one way toward a true self-governance: in the inter-workings of public stewards, not for mutual benefit alone, but on behalf of the whole, to the fullest measure of their joint interests and capacities. In small groupings, based upon an ethos of public stewardship, in a loose federation of autonomous colonies, in trade agreement, working in concert with existing governments and corporations, it is conceivable that provisional forms of self-management, orchestrating cultural affairs, a cooperatively-based economics and a material reserve system, can so regulate its own liberties and limitations to affect a better balance of power between the constituent members of its body.

Now that's a mouthful, so let's break it down.

III.

First, let's go back to basic principles:

We are all (presumably) agreed that governments derive their powers from the consent of the governed; that the purpose of elections is principally to secure the unalienable rights of the individual; "that among these are Life, Liberty and the pursuit of Happiness." Noble words ... that, however, don't mean diddly squat if in the same breath we condone the apparently ulterior motive of free enterprise: namely, the survival and advancement of the financially fittest. So little credence is given to the *quality of life* of the individual, in the dog-eat-dog pursuit of mangy money, that the rights of life, liberty and happiness are rendered nearly null and void -- or so watered down in generality as to be meaningless. For what is the "right to life" if there is not implied a guarantee that every man, woman and child is entitled to the basic *necessities* for a meaningful existence? What is "liberty" to a population so entrained on the treadmill of monotony and near poverty as to be denied any real *choices?* What is "happiness" to a dead routine that cannot get a whiff of satisfaction and joy but briefly through some superficial entertainment? (I do not count "job satisfaction" as an honest human emotion.)

If the "pursuit of happiness" is universally rendered as nothing more than the "pursuit of money," it is no wonder that every nation hemorrhages from the same gaping wounds of self-inflicted stupidity. The unabridged pursuit of rank and stuffing will never plug those holes, or compensate for the absence of an abdicated brain.

47

Remember, we are not exactly trying to reinvent a nation, or resolving a grand theory of economy. We are only trying to conceive a template for a colony: to understand the dynamics of a self-governing group to arrive at a provisional framework that can be modelled to the surrounding community. In the larger society, which has not yet got its mind wrapped around the concept of sovereignty, "Government" and "Greed" and "God" are something of a three-headed dragon, an *external* dynamic that basically seems to lord it over the puny individual, who feels his or her life basically circumscribed and regulated. But in a self-governing group (where membership participates to an appreciable degree in its own decision-making) each member *is* that dragon. That simplifies things considerably ... except that it frightens the hell out of everybody.

In considering the dynamics of a self-governing group, straightaway we can dispense with the whole notion of representation, or the delegation of privilege and responsibility *carte blanche*. The "dragon" of personal power is *internal* to every steward. *Sovereignty*, not some delegated authority, is the operating dynamic. Indeed, we can largely dispense with the notion of a seated government: an *open forum* is all that is needed. We are not even looking for a framework of *colonial* government or economy or society; we are pointing up the fact that a truly sovereign colony grows its own distinctive framework organically; it defines *itself*, out of what it innately *is*. The leadership and the following are one and the same.

A cooperative colony is a kind of entity in its own right -- a social *organism,* with a will and a yearning of its own: the sum of its participating parts. In a representative democracy (also a social organism, just less obvious because of its impersonality), responsibilities in decision-making are necessarily delegated away; there is very little societal participation. And where goes an individual's responsibility, so goes the individual's *ability to*

48

*respond:* that is to say, his *destiny.* Now he must do as he's *told.* And that is the slow undoing of any mentality.

Leadership is a privilege. A privilege can be abused. A privilege retained is called an "unalienable *right.*" An "unalienable *right,*" by definition, cannot be taken away. On this we have a consensus. A government merely reflects that consensus, or lack of same. A frightened individual will consent to anything. That's called a citizenry. A sovereign is no citizen. A sovereign is a molder of clay. A molder of clay is a maker of almost anything.

The whole notion of formal government, from a colonial perspective, is passé; for where a sovereign presides, no government is necessary.

Now we're getting down to the nitty-gritty of self-governance. A nation implies a *general* consensus. A colony is more specific. A large society functions via "due process" to the bindings of civil or statutory law. A stewardship is pure civility. A self-governing group has no buffer to cushion a self-assertion, nothing to hide behind, no circumlocution to disguise a crime. A legislature,... well....

Anyone can presume to speak for the will of "the People," and "the People" my go along with it for an agreeable spell, if the goals and rules are reasonably well disguised or well-intentioned. But by and by the enchantment wears thin, reality sets in, and lame excuses cease to cover up all the bare facts and rhetoric they used to. Sooner or later the build-up of laws will preempt a constitution, lawmakers now representing different and dubious interests; a republican jargon still rolls from the tongue, but the democratic speech is just an addiction. And when no other group can speak adequately and honestly for a disenchanted people, and leadership is just a damned bureaucracy, what is to become of a headless people?

49

A tongue-wagging president is not "the People." No senator, no representative, no candidate, administrator, officer, director, manager, CEO, priest or preacher, has ever yet spread a mind out so continental. No newspaper, no talking head on a television spouting "News You Can Trust" to steer your sons and daughters with. Only a self can speak for a self. All else must be, of necessity, in some way or other biased and bigoted. This writing of mine can be no different. We are necessarily limited to our own perspectives and ulterior motives. An individual can no more speak adequately for *all* "the People" than all "the People" can speak adequately for Itself.

The best guessed estimates of *common law,* hammered out in small-group leaderships before an open forum of would-be brothers -- these have ever been the surest safeguards against the mob on the one hand and cabals of private interest on the other. A nation is always too big for its britches. There is just no substitute for representation in self-government than a common willingness to simply lend a hand where needed, and the common sense to recognize the moment when it comes for speaking up or laughing out loud "We the People" is only an abstract idea; and a regional congress is a poorly kept Secret. It's not until we put our *own* heads together in the only way possible -- as sovereign individuals, *self*-representative -- that we come to know ourselves in a tangible form; a social organism that *can*, by God, begin to speak for Itself in the only speech it can, the only speech humanly possible: the speech of mind to mind and man to man; of woman to woman, of man *and* woman; of cell to cell: the speech of mouth to mouth and hand to hand. There is seldom sincerity in any other. We are all basically liars: we have to have the truth wrestled out of ourselves.

## IV.

I am not insensitive to the fact that there is a certain futility in offering even a general blueprint for a more direct form of democracy such as I suggest; that the novelty of "recolonizing our communities" will seem ludicrous to some, charming but impractical to others; that the mere mention of adjusting the lawmaking mechanisms of our courts and legislatures and executives is liable to make some people pass out cold. Obviously no one is going to take the ball and run with it. The beauty of my social vision is that *no one has to do anything about it!*

So there must be some other purpose in offering these thoughts, and there is. It is to suggest that the "recolonization of our communities" and the "reclamation of forgotten rights" and the "reconstruction of broken things" are already taking place. It is endemic to evolution, it just goes by other names.

And there is a value in understanding this: that our civilization is not entirely in the hands of mediocre politicians and would-be presidents; and constructive changes are not left to the devices of radicals and malcontents. *Outwardly* we may have only a paltry *vote* with which to make amends, and no real candidates that inspire honest confidence, only the lowest common denominator to waste it on; but *inwardly* something else operates in the minds of men and women; in the evolution of social organisms. We have not come to the ends of science, philosophy, *or* religion. The gradual development and awakening of the latent potentials of the mind does not depend upon a public initiative. It *is* initiative. It operates in us all the time. It raises man above the dreamtime of the apes. It is the *green* in all our grassroots efforts; the spiritual impulses that leap into flame of revolutionary inspirations from time to time. These are the adjutants that make possible the very *reality* of the mind. Whether we retain their astounding promptings, or slip into the

51

usual coma of a work-a-day routine, is a matter of prerogative and rather poor social clime.

Whatever may be said against us in our slow evolutionary ascent from servants to Sons, we are most astoundingly *creators in our own right*, however we choose to express or contain that rascally fire. It is, in part, the ministry of the adjutants that makes this so; that gives us the *potentiality* for logical, moral and venerable intelligence -- or what I call the three fiduciary powers of our mind endowment. But these three intuitions do not just *chance* to blossom into mid-conscious-ness. They are the "morontia fibers" -- the moral-ontological filaments of our inheritance -- *coaxed* into the intellectual twine of fine reasoning, and the tapestries of philosophy, and the "shrouds of turins": the worshipful revelation of our own sublime.

But there is a spiritual origin -- a Source -- of this mid-mind region. *Potentiality* implies *pattern,* and neither of these are acceptably "real" to the material mind. It must have its answers slapped in the face; it only accepts what is obvious to its five senses: it lives in a "five-cents world." But to the higher mind, registering frequencies at the superconscious level, potentials are *actuals*; and that world is just too damn rich and lavish for the nickel-and-dimer. But the "soul" -- the mid-mind -- is the accomplishment of long experience *between* the two extremes of the material world and the spiritual. We are the upgrowth of intrinsic designs, of *potential pattern.* These are the interworking of potentials in logic and morality and sublimity that, by and by, yield to us our fiduciary powers. Collectively, we hurl this out into vast enterprises -- the fiduciary branches of our civil, religious, and corporate governments and committees: executives, legislatures, and judiciaries. It belies the truth of all that we embody, for nothing grows but from the *inside* out. Which is to say that Christ was right: the "kingdom of heaven" only swells *out*; and the Arch-Fiduciary is the Father-indwelling of his own kind.

In the end, I cannot, and would not if I could, offer a concrete framework for small-group leadership. Anything that we currently have will work just fine. I have a vague idea that leans against the wind, in the direction of simple decency and practical expediency. I am a rhyming man without a single friend, who longs to know and weighs the would-be wealth of these; or say I'm a home-grown philosopher with a *world* of friends. Same thing. This is my offering nonetheless. A concept of public stewardship; a dream of colonies; a pocketful of nouns and adjectives. A self-educated grasp still groping after Sovereignty. I will have more to say about these. I am a man of a thousand itches. I scratch my pen over everything. Much remains unsaid. We will always be strangers, you and I. But I cannot shake hands with a government. I have never even *seen* a representative. I am not one to give away my consent so lightly to anyone. I am my own government. I am my own president.

I regard you the same.

*Like hardened fingers to a little hand,*
*Thus does Almighty God*
*Stretch the limits of our understanding*
*His Almighty Man.*

**- Cantos from the Ghost of Lincoln**

*"The chief difference between men and angels is that a man 'occupies' space, where an angel permeates it. Man, of course, in his own higher frequency range, also permeates his clump of space, but in his intense identification with it -- in his focalization upon the electrochemical functions that render him spiritually blind -- he seems rather to displace energy than to receive, store, and project it; which is, of course, the more accurate picture. But a circuit- breaker is also a circuit-maker. You are now embarked upon a course of training; and in the long years of that training, like generations of cadets before you, you will by slow, painstaking degrees become less stultified, less coagulate; more 'liquid' and 'mercurial' in your musings. You are the chromatin in the cells of the social organism, saturated with informations of intelligence and light. Study well the techniques of divinity, and the value of the imprints you imbibe from all of your encounters in the mind-space of reflectivity, and you too will join the corps of those living mirrors of space and the jumpers of time, and aid in the ongoing restoration of the circuits of inter-planetary and interdimensional association. You have embarked upon the Great Fight."*

Astari Manuscript, Book I,
*Fragments from the First Academy Archives.*

* * * * * * *

## Essay 3:

## Little Brown Toes in a Terrible Fear of Stomping.

In previous essays, I spoke of a "quiet revolution" -- a rather grandiloquent way of saying that increasing numbers of people are waking up to a sense of personal empowerment; questioning the basic tenets of science and religion alike, which either denies the existence of a higher stratum of conscious-ness, or forbids any exploration of it; that in either case, the substantive basis of individual consciousness goes ignored. I said that sooner or later it is inevitable that a shift in power must occur between the self-actuated sovereignty of the individuals and their delegated representatives. I suggested the possibility of a loose federation of colonies to facilitate that shift, and offered a lot of agitating words toward the end of highlighting aspects of a provisional framework for said colonies. I spoke of self-governing groups as social *organisms* growing out of what they innately *are*; that a given colony must define itself, a *living* framework more than a thing incorporated. I spoke of "stewardship" as a public ministry; of "common law" as a counterbalance to parchment law; of the need for "Codicils."

In this present meandering, I will revisit these ideas and carry them forward.

I.

Before we can speculate upon what is sure to become a very interesting clash between colonial "common law" and existing "statutory laws," we must probe further into the very basis of *all* laws -- written or implied -- in the nature of nature itself; *human* nature in particular, though we must acknowledge a common Source to all natural phenomena, whatever *that* may be. Religion and science are generally disagreed.

I would build a better bridge between the soul and body if I could, for it would shore up a thousand points of error; but I am straining at my capacities. Between the enigma of the "soul" and the embodiment of a "mind", I know only of a gulf that spans the length of my being, and errors or no, what planks and gaps of understanding bridge me sole to soul will have to hold.

I know that one cannot go forward who is too strongly doubtful; that labor must have meaning, and a life its purpose. I know that the pursuit of an ideal, against the backdrop of the ordinary and "real", the monotony of conformity, can lead one

58

into grave dissatisfactions with oneself, one's culture, one's people, till only the so-called "status quo" is seen, and the ideal in comparison becomes all the more impossible. I have been down inside that pit of self-disdain, blind to all but what I found distasteful. I smelled but my own vomit on the world, had become too morally self-righteous and puritanical. In such a quandary, I came to understand that if a good proportion of humankind felt deceived, I was the more deceitful. Yet in crawling upon my belly self-ashamed, I became all the more acquainted with the down-and-out, the disenfranchised and resentful. Human nature sneaks to be so crudely shit upon. I looked for culprits, and found us at our TVs, cowering in the shadows of our pixels and pulpits.

When we give too much credence to such hypothetical nonsense as a human "machine"; to the ancient concept of "original sin"; to an overly practiced dogma of vulnerability to terrorists and disease -- then we become a society hypnotized by ancestral achievements and idiocies. We rob ourselves of our innate dignity for that which smears it; forget that we also stand upright as men and women; that even the children of our foes are innocent. The poor befuddled adult spends all the day repenting, feeling sorry for itself, and sorely afraid for its longevity and its salvation; stands illegitimate before a mirror, before a friend. We were happiest when we were children, for we had not yet learned to stand condemned. What conclusion, then, but that embryos make the happiest citizens! We denizens of the waking world are tangled up in "-isms."

We send our representatives to go make laws for us; mountains of them; whole *walls* of them, to hem us in lest we do some primate damage to ourselves. They dutifully pretend. (They are really making loopholes for their friends.) We look forlornly through imaginary bars, "pray do not feed the animals," and contemplate the convolutions of our undeservabilities. I try, but I cannot take us very seriously. We are so damn cute and cuddly, down on all fours, lolling in our industries.

I am aware that not all people hate their jobs; that not all people so despise themselves that they cannot stand the sight of other people (looking at them); that not everyone feels their life is meaningless, or hollow, or shallow; not everyone lacks a purpose; and not all people are dissatisfied with the so-called "status quo" -- of which there is not really any: all are individual; all are sifting through their options, choosing their potential. The social disgruntlement I focus on is through the lens of my *own* disgruntlement. I have a vision of things to come I want to show; and many things that stand or lean right where they are I find too antithetical. I am something of a literary bully: I charge out on the playground knocking other bullies sensible. I stomp on marbles. I scan the horizon like some Daniel Boone; I keep my scalp. I will blaze a trail through such a wilderness that even my state senator can pass. But here where I am, statutory laws are rather cumbersome than useful. There are too many strings attached. It makes my mulishness uncomfortable. And I have only a very skinny ass for such a load of ... well ... I would rather make up my own mind, and stand on my own principles, than be herded through some civics lesson in too much pride of partial checks and balances squandered from a pile of people.

So all huzzahs to those who are having a wonderful time, blessed be their titles. But there are two sides to a coin, and I am weighing the relative values of the whole. A civilization is not *all* fun and games; it is also half miserable. Let us amuse ourselves and go explore the strange anomalies of this peculiar carnival.

Societies are essentially organized by their dreams, regulated by their code of ethics. These find expression in the laws -- whether written or assumed -- giving us all the varied facets of church, state, corporation, school, home, machine. By our common and statutory rules we regulate our minds in search of our ideals. All of our social agreements and behaviors may be said to serve this dual purpose. Basically, it all comes down to what is allowed (more or less specific) and what is generally frowned upon or disallowed (not always so specific). Then, of course, there is that which is just taken anyway. For simplicity's sake: there are paths laid down, and deviations more or less tolerable.

But underneath and around and permeating all these bylaws by which we govern and regulate ourselves -- our thinking, our behaviors, our relations -- there are obviously "natural laws" that make our myriad regulations possible to begin with; indeed, our very existence. No discussion of law and order, or of any manner of reform, would be complete without reference to our dependency on this foundation. It is the basis, not only of our physiology, but of our *thinking*. That is, we are able to *think up* such concatenations of philosophy and expediency as we do because we are innately *built* in such a way that it comes natural: body and mind so overlap and interpenetrate that we can avoid a host of errors by regarding the two as one. I am not only so obviously what I *am*, but what I *think* I am: my bits and pieces, and all that holds them more or less together.

When I say "natural law", I do not mean simplistically the laws of gravity or magnetics, *per se.* Science likes to thumb its marbles, but that is a silly game. What mere mechanistic thinking regards as mechanical *forces*, we who must use *all* our brains experience as *psychological momentum.* Nature must have a Source, be that what it may, which we can only know as "self" and that which in-forms and out-flows as a self-*reality,* to which we like to give godzillion names to make ourselves more prideful of a change. We have not figured anything out, just re-arranged our living rooms, but we like the sensation of having moved a *something.*

61

That essentially gives us a sovereign base in self, inside a little bubble we like to call "Reality." That is enough for some, until a crisis comes; and then we are compelled by some pointy necessity to speculate upon the *Source* of all our troubles. Now we are really in trouble, because we must pop the bubble in which we are so uncomfortably ensconced, and we are mortally afeared to be without our bubble even for a nanosecond of existential treason. (That means: we do not really like to reason except in little circles.) By and by we manage to get a thought thunked out, and, lo and behold! -- with all that huffing and puffing and justifying our complaints, we begin to discover a Self *within* the self, and another *Bubble!* Now we are feeling like Lawrence Welk -- sublimely "Wunnerful!" -- for we have discovered a something Else!

But here is where all hell breaks loose and worlds collide, for we cannot quite get our minds wrapped around that Bubble of something Else; but we have laid out a logical path that plainly shows the whole world where the Smartest Brain That Ever Lived is standing at ... but no two geniuses ever quite agree, for they have laid out different tracks! The Mystery of the Bubble, in all this warp and woof, is simplified into a Tapestry ... on which we wipe our feet.

Thus, the "Spirit" of a reverential attitude devolves into a terrible Face, until the Terror of the multitude becomes too terrible to believe, becomes so laughable that just to keep one's head on straight the whole idea of a God is exchanged, like a burned-out bulb, for a less intimidating and more illuminating magnetosphere.

Bless our little hearts, but we are so phenomenally stupid. We are just neatly dividing our peas and mashed potatoes to opposite sides of the plate: we still have to eat 'em. If we are not separating all our goods from all our evils (positive and negative poles of force, for those more robotic), we are probably sliding asleep at the table, already dreaming.

I prefer to call this "Reality" scheme a Magnificent Bubble. I imagine this first as a peacock-colored aura surrounding my body like an Oval Office; which is to say, I give credence to the colors of my disreputable emotions, as being necessary articles of my mental clothing, for I feel naked and embarrassed with just my skinny reason. After this, of course, comes the bubble of the atmosphere, and everybody knows about the in-out breathing of molecules by which we build up bone and muscle of ourselves out of ... well ... *air!* (This is the part where "Spirit" becomes just plain ole "Breath," and "soul" becomes machine, and "consciousness" becomes unthinkable.) But then my robotic circuitry informs me of yet another layer: a magnetic bubble around the Earth, by which those molecules are called and held to order, in a seánce room called a "cellular congress," where the DNA presides as the Speaker of the House, and laws are passed from hand to hand like a bottle of colored water.

I suppose most of us think of the conscious mind as a lump or a cloud, not taking the time to consider that when we factor it out of our equations, it becomes (for us) an Outside thing, like a terrible God, or a force of nature. But then all we have done is to pit ourselves against each other within the confines of a vicious dogma, eating a soupy porridge of scientific and religious who-knows-what, damned by our own diet of what passes for a fluffy faith or a bloodless logic. We tend to cage ourselves in either a moral or intellectual rigidity; or, fleeing these entrapments, we run like hell for the nearest exit to their opposites.

As individuals, we're only trying to keep some semblance of integrity, searching for balance by running back and forth between extremes. As societies, we tend to clump up shoulder to shoulder in trying to be the first one through the door. This is called a social order. And like all orders, it's enough to make you scream.

A conscious mind is a nation's best and most abundant natural resource. But it is not a "thing" to be mined, like lime, or hoarded like marbles. There can be no shortage of consciousness, only redundancy of usage. There can be insecurity, and thus a fear of extravagance. There can be a yearning for liberty, and thus a lavishness. But when we overlook the obvious, that we have but to *think* to experience our own replenishment, then we can act like puppets, and come to believe that someone else's hand controls our fate; some God, or Chance, or a self-proclaimed spokesman for a theoretical universe. I personally cannot distinguish between all that we grope to define as natural and spiritual. We are too quick to draw lines. A Stream flows through us, *IS* us, that is both hormone and odyssey, and we are both wise beyond measure and utterly clueless. Yet it is from this base that we argue for our potentials or for our limits, solidify them into codified systems, and wonder why the half of us are idolized as being all but chiselled in place, while the rest of us are feeling whipped and shoeless, standing in a line with a long, long face.

I do not mean to tread underfoot all the relics of old arguments we tend to hold polished and sacred. I am, instead, artfully charming the bright green snake from a hole in the ground of our thinking, for a new genesis. We are in many ways grown too afraid of ourselves, too superstitious. Do we really need stone commandments for seatbelts? Must we be so afraid of a god coming out of a hypothetical sentence? I understand that all our laws and dogmas and highbrow glances are meant to proclaim ourselves as being in effort of mostly innocence. What I don't understand is nanny government, and the psychological stacking-up of so much self-resistance. We are not *exactly* living in a land of the free anymore. We are electronically hungry and hunkered down in a maze of theoretical trenches. We are scratching at lice in our brains. We point our fingers like rifles, but faint at the mention of cannons.

Yet, for all of this, we are rather simple. We are not as caged and circumscribed by limitations as we believe. We are just overly or underly scruppled. If we do not live large, to the perimeters of our most continental dreams, it is probably just that we aim too much to please.

There is a balance to be sought on any given theme, according to individual inclination and learning. It is only when we cannot make up our own minds that we get crosswise of ourselves and abdicate our intuitions. The preacher, sorely self-oppressed, finds solace with his mistress; the mistress discovers something sacred in her service. Collectively, democracy is sleeping with its representatives. We despise ourselves and adore each other; or we despise each other and adore ourselves: it is difficult to tell with so many people piling up on both ends of the teeter-totter.

I am not suggesting that we hang the rules. I am suggesting that we put our heads together. The rate of legislation in a country indicates a people too afraid to guide and trust *themselves*. Its leadership must do *all* the thinking; and one mind cannot carry a million selves without dropping *something*.

We are a nation of laws only for lack of being a nation of *wills*.

II.

There are those who simply prefer the rigid structure of formal rules. They are not imbeciles. They are just too tightly or too loosely self-governing. It simplifies everything to be told what to do and when to do it; to have excuses to avoid full self-responsibility as sovereign entities facing a lonely forbidden. We pay our taxes, pay our tithes, earn our pittance, spend our lives. We are generally extending ourselves and our treasures less that we like to admit it; but, hey, we try. We have evolved a lazy tolerance for strings and conditions: in love, in art, in law; in science and religion; in work and play. We are somewhat like little kittens, in that a tangle of yarn will usually suffice for lack of a grander yard. We are not exactly without a sense of purpose, it is just that we have never had to catch a mouse all by ourselves, from having grown up in and acclimated to the kitchen. The Great Big Woods outside our bounds have scarcely come to our attention.

There is a patch of green, I'm told, for just such kittens. Some are calling it (rather blandly) an unplanted future. Others are calling it Armageddon. I am still bushwacking here, and getting welts across the face and a blur to vision, so pardon my imagination if I am seeing a mildly wild and unfettered nation, or a tribal sovereignty, or a federation of muddy colonies, still wet with dreaming up its possibilities and joint intentions.

I am trying to feel and intuit my way into that space that I am calling a cooperative colony, a stewardship, a village sovereignty, a Vision; to find new planks of thought to reason with, that could make direct democracy and a fair economy real enough to mold between participating minds, who do not shrink from getting in-tu-it. I am wise enough to know that anatomy begins with a mind: in those exquisite imbalances of electrical exchange between the ethereal glow and the particle chain that we call the molecular human. We mimic the very same in the larger social organism. But not yet comprehending the details of this, we tend to cluster into churches and machines and all manner of little boxes, swinging like monkeys from cage to cage, cunning as mobsters, caught in extremes, defending our goods and evils, offending our own senses. We cannot seem to make our own two ends meet, thinking back-and-forth as we do on a mile-long line. We are basically chain-ganged for fear of being too independent, and only put our heads together to cry.

We could learn a lot from a hydrogen bond, small as it is; not only how to put our heads together and get along, but how to show initiative; how to compound mutual interests in simply looking from eye to eye; how to string ourselves along as ornately as a molecular government, a single organism billions of craniums strong: out of the muck of our myriad differences, One Dignity, an enlightened Animal, a humane humanity, eighty-four-thousand centuries long.

(Give or take a millennium.)

I am aware that no one in their right mind can take me seriously. And no one in their left mind knows what I'm talking about. I am too surgical and nebulous. I am terminally poetic, still playing with my rhymes. But "reality" is conjured out of just such electrical bits in the quantum spaces of our neuronets, where past and future meet. This moment of your reading me, you are stretching out like a bridge between synaptic tips. You are contemplating your scaffolding. Collectively, we think we are contending with the disappointments of our wrap-around environments. Really we are engineering possibilities. I am an enigma to those who are lounging in the shade of overgrowths and perfect theories, chewing on their sandwiches. But we are all of us Enigmas. We span the gulf between our hardcore facts and our invisibilities. Eat your sandwiches. I am just drumming on your thinking caps, making a nuisance of myself between the pleasant pauses of my sentences. You cannot fire me. Get used to it. Tonight is a long time coming, when we can stretch ourselves out long before the nubile landscapes of our televisions, reflecting upon our wants and grievances, to process our emotional addictions, a little ashamed of ourselves, stuttering forward by remote control. Everything we know comes down to moments too electrical.

I am pushing every button on the console of my mind. There is a vision in my frontal lobe, in nanosecond time, that does not jive with anything I'm being told. Religion is a farce that tends to rob me of my dignity, offering some salvation in a bloody bowl. It convolutes my common sense, crucifies my soul (still hung up there after twenty centuries of the same old telling). The evening news is selling so much dirty laundry, just another kind of infomercial, doling out indulgences in the form of pharmaceuticals. I vomit up my spleen just trying to get it down. The marketplace is always offering one or another pretty thing, but I find too much technology, will all its tinkering and technical thinking, deadly cold. I am not really complaining; I like a carnival as much as anyone. But there is only so much cotton-candy I can hold. I have more appetite for Life than anything I am being sold.

I must be getting old.

I'm sitting on a park bench looking at the world through dusty spectacles, accumulating friends in the form of pigeons on my shoulders; they are eating bread crumbs from my hands. Yes, it's hard to believe, but I'm already fifty-one-and-some-odd-centuries old.

I find I'm not content with small-talk anymore. I mind my rope and well. I know the world is thirsty. Now and then a soul comes at me with a swinging bucket, and I want to pour an ocean out and fill them up with liquid luck, with everlasting overfill, as much as we can handle between two helpful selves. We chat about the weather; whether or not the geese will come, or take a wrong turn over Albuquerque, what with La Niňa and El Niňo taking turns directing cloud traffic over the Pacific. Nevermind the mud below, new green will grow. I send them home bent over left or right with more than skinny arms can lift up over a mile. But one by one they all come back, swinging an empty thimble. We're learning how to think and be, in the way we like to repeat ourselves. The future is under our very feet, in the overspill between the giving and receiving; in the way we seed and water our labor of learning how to share ourselves.

I am no anarchist, and no utopian. I am simply taking a roundabout way of suggesting we put our crayons together and draw up a plan for ourselves in the form of Codicils. I am a proud and imperfect man, but I have not yet found anyone clever enough to govern me as well and honestly as I govern myself. Angel or no, my government begins and ends with me. I am a sovereign entity, and coming to know the scope of what that means, from the height of God to the depth of doubt, encompassing all my wealth and poverty. No priest can speak for me; no scientist undermine my immortality; no politician oversee and overlight me. No master who does not shoulder with me will employ me. And no one who can stand my company will long worship me. Though I be a bastard of the universe, I shake hands. And I will speak bibles if I have to in making my amends. I grow beastly under the yoke of laws, but tame me to a few fair friends, and simple codicils will do to guide me.

I understand how lavish a table I must seem to spread out over the noses of so many ants. The simple fact is, we are acclimated to our servitudes. We are uncertain of our spiritual roots. We live in condemnation of ourselves for simply being human. We are too conscious of our lacks. We seem to think our lives are predetermined, if not by an ancient tribal deity, then by some glorified lab technician's convoluted theorem. We are sunk at every headline, law, and sermon; and reason from such chronic habits of lack-based thinking that we seem to have come unplugged from a wall. But *doubt* is the only wall there ever was. We were not *born* to be these head-shrunk dolls, standing slack jawed at our designated posts. Why, to walk away from a job is damn near treason! We allow our laws to proliferate without restraint, our Constitution to be preempted, while we're kept distracted -- and we are so distractable, so practiced at our mental habits -- we are set on automatic. Who needs television ... we are nanotubes. We are walking infomercials. We are selling tennis shoes on our jackets. It is no wonder to me that the notion of a sovereign colony, where people are expected to act like full grown humans, and *allowed* to be; to reason away their differences all by themselves, and build consensus; without false-representatives interfering with a sponsor's need to sell the whole world panic insurance, or what have you; it is no wonder to me that the notion of sovereignty is still so nebulous, so "not me", so shrugged off onto bigger shoulders. Do not be grieved. It is a natural phase of childhood to find ourselves turned coward. It is exactly what we have ever been trained to be. It is a mighty act to even contemplate a self-empowered freedom.

But we are sovereign entities nonetheless. Even diaper clad, in all the glory of our gibberish and our baby fat, we are that. So I will continue to blather on about this business of being truly human, until I have arrived at something resembling a masterpiece, if only from a sideways view. And I will lay it on as thick and bad as only my two halves of me and you can do.

We have got to get the wreck of church and science off our backs. These suffocate all reason in denying us our dignity, and insult like a knife the core of our intelligence. We have no choice but to ply our human traits. But as sons of a Father in our own right, potential godlings, with even the simple power to *think*; and by thinking so set forth the first reverberations of our makings. We are fools to give no credence to our boundless *minds*. We create. We cannot *not* create. Even before there is any physical evidence to convince our eyes, we set forth intentions in the flux of Life and follow in their wake; and flux of Life responds in kind at every particle, resonating to our every want, even when we sit on them with our complaints. We are not half as miserable as we pretend; we only frustrate all our effort of making new designs. We are supreme disturbers of environment: we agitate all microscopic things electrical to our probing minds; we only daydream, and the world coagulates around us; our signatures spike at every pulse, and like graffiti color everything. Are we too timid? Are we too bold? Are we forever getting in our way? In consciousness alone we are laying Roman roads, and nature sends us blatant revelations every day. Yet, look at us: we cower before bacteria for fear to catch a cold.

My argument (and it *is* an argument, believe it or not) may seem too metaphysical. But our very wants and needs are essentially metaphysical. *WE* are more than physical. It makes sense to *me* to reason from the source of things. A *lack-based approach* to any subject is fundamentally a feeding frenzy: a vying for attention to fill up a hole; or a self-defense of self-betrayal, having got ourselves convinced of being robbed, now standing with our pockets hanging out and feeling vulnerable. But a *source-based approach* to any subject is fundamentally a giveaway: a life self-generating; one who can afford to let go of a stingy need, or a reason for stubbornly being afraid. I call this kind of self-assurance (rather, a Source-assurance) the beginning of knowing what it is to be a "public steward." A "lacker" is essentially a boat with a hole in it; the slightest opinion could sink it, or tip it either way. These do not make good consensus-builders. The best use of a lacker's mouth is to put a finger in it. But a public spirited steward is a one-man ship of state: there is nothing like a source-awareness to put the wind in your sails. These make the best consensus-builders, for they are not hollow in the center, but always overflowing with a good idea to help another stop com-plaining and lend a hand in bending over to help another for a change.

71

Lackers tend to delegate the bulk of their decision-making (and thus their responsibilities) to the loudest taker, and thus tend to live in a cage -- a job, a house, a disease:  a hole by *any* name is still a hole -- and thereby end up with a mountain of regulations and petty fees and requirements, unnecessary and invasive policing, mandatory licensing and insurance, stone commandments, what have you, for all their troubles.  But stewards are not very big on delegating.  They tend to wing it on their own expertise, while the doubters are doubting with a "let's wait and see" every cloud coming with a potential disease, an act of God, or a disapproving sneeze from a local congress. Lackers for laws, and stewards for ease, do not mix well in any setting, basically.

But let's not get too far out ahead of ourselves, for we are all of us, probably, lackfully oriented more than we want to admit it; and, no doubt, public spirited with a breeze in our sails more often than we want to notice.  We care more than we let on; we couldn't care less if we push it.  I am not recruiting a membership, lamenting the lack of stewards; I am just wishing there were more of us.  (See what I mean?)

The codicils for a new genesis will arise from what we are, when little by little we learn the value of putting our own heads together, not to merely cast a vote yea or nay, or to hang a representative, but to build consensus.  I foresee a day when our defensiveness of all our insecurities will come crashing down.  Already we pay little heed to CEO's and presidents and other chiselled heads:  we make our own way through the labyrinth they impose.  Some of them are decent.  Some of them deceive themselves far more than we need give them any credence.  They are pullers of strings, and puppets themselves, and they cannot but know it in honest moments.  But that is *their* shame and slow undoing.  We have our own nets to mend, and getting to it.

III.

Any group that functions under statutory laws has put itself in a precarious position, for the very act of putting oneself under another's authority implies an abdication of personal right and responsibility in exchange for bully protection and privilege. Authoritarian control then preempts private mobility and discretion to one degree or another, depending upon the extent of the trade-off between master and governed, and how the balance of power between authority and servitude snowballs. It's like a handshake between a robot and a child, that starts out okay, until a faulty program computes a need for more hydraulics, and that is the beginning of the end. Authority inevitably squeezes what it can to serve its own ends, and society incrementally weakens in the iron hand of its own devising. Political machinery does not compute a scream; and a population squeezed to eke a living is a flattened hand -- a passive repetition. It has no stomach for up-rising.

Can a society function without stone commandments? It all depends on the qualities of its people, doesn't it? And now we're back to human nature, and perceptions of ignorance and weakness. *And perception is the name of the game.* More specifically, the *perception of power*, and the lack of same.

At the present stage, it is unthinkable that a large society can function harmoniously without policing, for the mass perceptions of individual power are so convoluted, finding expressions in such extremes -- from violence and thievery to a downright spineless conformity and passivity -- that governments and governed alike often seem more or less out of their minds. A vicious cycle of reprisal and preemptive thinking, like a bull by its own tail, encircles everything. But at the basis of it all is a perception of powerlessness, that manifests as either an unoffending submissiveness, or a lashing-out of pent-up aggression or deviousness that perceives no better road. For

73

lack of understanding the certain fundamentals of human nature, many people would sell their souls for even a whiff of federal protection, or the talismanic superstition invoking angels from crucifix and crystal and essence of geranium to ward off the latest hobgoblins of New Aging Christian. The fart of a gun is another such potion, for those who have nowhere else to run, no recourse but to get their hands on *something*. All in all, we have taken self-measure and found ourselves wanting, now reduced to little brown toes in a terrible fear of stomping.

A state-granted *privilege* is an authorization, not an *unalienable right*. And bully protection is for the weak, who are already conquered by a self-perception: that nothing resides in them of any strength. Yet one has but to *think*, and something "magical" occurs at every synapse of the brain, that largely goes unrecognized: *a stream of consciousness collapses into particles that gives full-on sensory perception of a generated field of Mind, that we experience tangibly as environment.* "Reality" is a wrap-around hologram that we conjure for ourselves from our own intake. This is my understanding of the very *essence* of an individual's sovereignty: that we live what we live by focusing it into tangibility. And we blink it away at risk of making an unfortunate mistake.

Call it magic, call it science, call it spirituality, call it anything you like. I call it going from the hazy and generalized to the more specific. God-Outside, or that omniscient Instinct that dotes on the strong and ignores the weak, are both poorly thought-out plans toward our blindly going extinct. Every living thing, if it's living *something*, might as well be squirting ink! Isn't that damned obvious by now? What else could we mean by "living" but that anything that shows a vital sign of being *alive* must "live" on juice of *something*, both in mode of receiving from the Stream of Life, and in contributing. How that Stream is then converted into mode of tangibility for the pearl of wisdom gleaned from the trials and errors of self-created experience -- is that not an accurate description of what we mean by "Life"?

So "power" is not intangible, it is just unrecognized. In fact, there is nothing experienceable *but* our placement in the Stream; our compression of variables into quantum beads, projecting these as landscape by and for a sovereign mind that knows itself as a "you" and an "I", like facets of a diamond, bedazzled in its own glory, or caught like a fly in the webworks of its own humility. "Power" need only be *perceived* to be exercised. It is not for lack of power that we stand self-deceived, but for our lack of understanding scope of mind. This is no cause for condemnation and casting blame on the blindness of our guides. All the trials of our lives are reducible to effort of learning. We are figuring all this stuff out, and well-being really does abound: it encapsulates and holds us up even in the passing moments of our diseases. There is no threat, no crime, no catastrophe we imagine but what we have support for all our trying. The very atoms of our knowing are intelligently coming and going. We are not ostracized: we are *becoming*.

IV.

My better value to humankind, I suppose, is basically that I tend to magnify. I am a grand exaggerator of the obvious, and I paint it thick. I am sometimes hard to understand, but only an idiot would try to bury such a big-headed bone as mine. For those who are only looking to complain, and equally for those who wish to understand and dream of knowing more, I offer scope for a ragged imagination. The landscape of social and political ills, on the one hand, and the mindscape of a neurosynaptic tip on the other hand, are to me about equally big. They are but two complementary ends of the same telescope, that only wants for an eye at either end. Looking out from an eye upon the boundless reaches of the cosmos, our daily

75

redundancies and entrapments are so minute as to hardly deserve a compliment. Looking inward from an eye upon the endless dots of our resourcefulness, I hardly know where to *begin* to compliment ourselves, for fear of falling in. Whatever wealth or poverty, whatever power of liberty or depravity, *whatever* fix we have got ourselves convinced that we are standing in, first exists in Stream and strata of mind. Every moment of our known existence, we have ever been the makers of time, the beginning of which is in any given moment, as small or as extravagant as we pretend: collapsing the All into pigment of light cast out into canvas of environment. If we are tired or angry or frightened of life, it is only from lack of experiment and redundancy of experience. Creation of life, by any terms, is a colossal chore of achievement. This is not blasphemy, to give open vent to innate divinity; try *not* to! Nor is it sedition against the state. It is called: Writing the Book of Genesis by Living It.

It is called: Building a Brain by Actually Using It.

Anyone can mind a stream of thought, collapse it into quantum particles, perceive it as moments of environment, and interact with their own redundancies made tangible in a 24-hour cubical. In fact, we are all doing just exactly that. We are so good at it by now, we run our minds on automatic; we are knocking about in our own rinse cycle. Permanently pressed. But most of us are so caught up in the Stream, living in circles, it seldom occurs to us to step back a bit to observe ourselves in the act of making conscious what is just a trickle. We are rather semi-conscious most of the time, more doodlers than actual artists; or accidentally conscious more often than on purpose. We always surprise and delight ourselves when we get a bright idea thunked out several lifetimes after it was started; or when a fortuitous event unfolds straight out of the blue, after so much time has elapsed that we plumb forgot that that was where we threw it. We tend to think of life as something that "just happens." But nothing sticks until we glue it: we get exactly what we concentrate on ... we just have a short attention span. And, forgive me for saying it, but we're rather addicted to our points of view. We tend to give the bulk of our attention to things unwanted, so present and real and proof to our senses, which keeps everything we know to be true and real so locked in place; we're creatures of habit; and worse: *creators* of habits. In light of all that we are so proudly entrained to embellish, the future barely rates our attention: it's just a cartoon.

But one who has learned the value of concentration upon an ideal is a pioneer on the only frontier there ever was: a meaningful moment. Anything less -- an "act of God", a "random occurrence" -- is a self-defecating affront to logic. It cleaves a mental kingdom in half to deny one's Source; and then there is only a concentration on habit. Religion as a clubfoot, and amputated science, will never pave the way for we who walk as giants.

I try to imagine a future time when all of this is common knowledge; when days are like cups overflowing, and even the froth of dreaming matters; when weeks are experienced by the flowering of a myriad things brought relatively effortlessly to some fruition, not as a cage of forty hours; when a month is rather like an open prairie, and another year older is but a further range. Collectively, nothing now seeming so permanent and overpowering will then even draw the gaze. Oh, we will have our problems, the lack of things just barely sensed, the powerful wanting of possibilities not yet as evident as prior wantings already standing in their open graves. Time is always marching forward with its new brigades. But we as the *makers* of time, shaving more meaningful moments from more fruitful brains, mental acuities sharpened like colored pencils in sketching tomorrow on a page, we are the determiners of our future fates; and the patterns of our living *then,* for all our deadly and colorful mistakes, will be the first perfectings of masterful strokes, that are but tracings of imaginings on the whiteness of today.

Time is only the neurological stuttering forward at the synaptic speed of today. But we are soft-wired. Time is pliable. It can be bent and tweaked and routed through the mid-mind, and give us alterations of environment at mere millivolts of speed. But not if we define ourselves merely as someone else's works of clay.

What a legacy we leave behind for those who follow after. If we today but *dream* of making such a use of mind, what landscapes must be springing from our loins; what colossal minds. In a few generations, humankind will be something other than it is today. We are the bridgers over all this current social decay, like an artist between canvases, cleaning up a messy yet somewhat productive day. We are the first generation of what will be the old advancers, we who currently and casually pave the way. We stride across this old terrain like atlassers. We may be but its first practicers, but what we collapse in our brains today, hurling out cathedral shapes to smash like avalanchers all the ugly structures standing in our way, tomorrow will breed human beings that gaze upon the world as masters.

So we have our work cut out for us.

The greater value of this manifesto is not so much in laying out particulars of a provisional framework for a hypothetical colony, although that is somewhat part of my aim. It is rather more importantly valuable in pointing up the reality of individual domain. In the little space that remains for this essay, I have only room to *hint* of that quality of mind I call "public stewardship," and of what I foresee as a greater reliance upon *common law* practices in hacking out a more equitable living in future "colonies," call them what we may.

A colony derives its existence from consensus-building and cooperation in industry and economics; but all talk devolves into defensiveness and manipulation if stewards are insufficiently sensitive to, and confident of, their sovereignty; if they are yet too lackfully oriented, and thus distrustful and unforgiving. They will just be trying to *fill up a hole* of one kind or another, like so many decision-makers today, not really focused securely in *adding to a whole*. I suppose this is inevitable, for we are only *beginning* to understand the power of mind in collapsing the Stream into engrams of perception that gives us environment: that is, we are yet *passive* perceivers. Until there is evidence of individual power in terms of manifestations, and thus private *confidence* in such ability, there will continue to be the lingering ghosts of doubts, the paralysis of fears -- dreamers and planners, but rather feeble *builders*, with nothing tangible in hand. It will take some time and practice to really "get it" that the principal medium of creation is *consciousness*, not economics. Collectively collapsing the Stream into tangible resources -- that is not only a trick of thinking, but a trick of *conversation*, to master.

I, personally, don't give a hoot about "reinventing govern-ment" or distributing cans to the needy. That all sounds rather boring, and in the long haul unnecessary. But there is always the question of equitability: things must get made and put into the hands where they are needed; but it is always better when those hands themselves are doing the building, in concert with a mind tending well to its own materials. A moment consciously intent upon genesis, that is what I call self-government and mutual economy. All else is redundant. We are poised at the beginning of what is sure to be a psychic *renaissance*, where attention to the internal Stream and our conscious intent in collapsing the "spiritual" into specifics of perception is the very essence of sovereignty. This will be a long time in learning; and this learning will often be set aside, in the heat of argument, for practical concerns over management and economy. We will talk like stewards long before we begin to act like them, for we have yet to fully comprehend how to stabilize the ethereal to the quantum. We have no choice, in coming together, but to reason from our individual instabilities. It is extremely difficult to share material resources in that context. *Hoarding* will be a chronic difficulty, when individuals can bring themselves to share at all. Perceptions of lack and distrust and insecurity run very, very deep; and actual *power* within the mind is difficult to comprehend and accept, let alone concentrate into environmental tangibility.

*"I had rather never learned to read and write
And cipher for myself, than call another mortal man
My statutory god."*

**Cantos from the Ghost of Lincoln.**

*"Needless to say, the development of the more expansive sensorium of modern times has not been without its chain of griefs. Like all evolutionary movements, human evolution has also had its share of monstrous mistakes. It has been the task of the Corps now for nearly two centuries to clean up these early evolutionary mastodons of our morontia space, and doubtlessly the massive cleanup effort of these domains will continue on for millennia. As a decimal world, a certain leeway has always been granted us by constellation authorities to deviate from the universal norms in our experimentation with the various echelons of image constructions. I need not tell you what a troublesome adventure this has been for the struggling civilizations of time; nor, on the other hand, what an evolutionary boon. Where would we be today, for example, without our intelligence corps of Manti, or the messenger services of the hordes of relay-types of imagery, or even of our 'watchdog' types? We have come a long way from the primitive days of our reliance upon man and machine. But the Borderland is still the Borderland, and broad sensorium or no, without continuing diligence and ethical protocols in the projection of our thought constructions, we will continue to hamper the integration of our circuitries into the mindspace of the Supreme Being of our local zones; which is, of course, our most ardent Hope."*

Astari Manuscript, Book III,
*Astronautical Summary of the Tripartisan Arena*.

\* \* \* \* \* \* \*

Essay 4:

# A Different Kind of Infinite.

My vision of a loose federation of cooperative colonies (essentially a network of "tribal sovereignties") functioning amidst and between existing communities, with their own individual styles of self-governance and economy, etc., yet working in concert with the surrounding society -- indeed, for the sole *benefit* of that society -- is an outrageous concept, perhaps, but nonetheless instructive for all its oddities. Some illuminating insights emerge from even contemplating such a possibility.

83

I.

It goes without saying that a tribal sovereignty comprised of impotents can hardly live up to its name; for then we have a group essentially frightened for its patchwork domain, worrying over every meal, and basically snarling over every bone that comes up for debate. So I have been primarily concentrating on the subject of sovereignty itself, which implies an *individual power* -- a subject most of us are rather nebulous about.

We *think* we've figured out the concept of "inalienable right," except that we have a dubious regard for the "subterranean" aspect of the human mind, which makes ourselves prime suspect in any question of liberty. Basically, we're not sure what we'll get up to if we break away from our constraints, so we tend to stay where we are told, and generally look for entertaining ways to keep ourselves sedate. In fact, so well are we entrained in our redundancies -- be it the drudgery of a daily grind, a chronic pain, or just a vague unsettled feeling that doesn't even rate a name -- I suspect that we are mostly utterly confused. Life used to be more promising, once upon a time; something we used to wake up looking forward to. That optimism still remains, I guess, more or less, give or take a few deep holdouts settled in our brains. Not everyone complains. Most everyone has something passing for spirituality, and that's a kind of pick-me-up supertonic for a scattered brain; but, in all honesty, it often seems to come so watered down in new and biblical clichés, it's basically fumes. I spray it in the air around me, but it smells of something cute or next-to-nothing, so I am terminally walking, walking, walking anywhere I can to get away.

A power without real substance is just talk of ... nothing. There is no power in a phrase.

So I have been exercising all two hemispheres of my worldly mind to come up with a bright idea to put down something meaty on our plate. Something to sink your teeth into. (I didn't have to kill anything, so it works for vegans too.) I introduced the concept of a substantive power in my last essay, and it bares repeating here, for it touches upon the very essence of an individual's sovereignty, which is the very basis of intrinsic rights, and gives effectiveness to our abilities. It is for lack of understanding this -- that we have a substantive power available to us at our own discretion to exercise -- that we have become so lackfully oriented in the scrap-heap of our lives, and tolerate the machinery of so many dubious authorities over-managing everything.

As near as I can state it in a simple formula, power functions in our lives in a cycle of consciousness that works something like this: we mind a stream of thought from consciousness-flow of All That Is, pulling in according to our thinking habits and preferences; synaptic firing collapses this harmonic stream into quantum particles (engrams of perception), which we perceive as moments of environment; emitting our responses back into the Stream. Basically, we draw from the whole to enrich the whole, and we are part of the Supreme Being who shares our evolution with us, *as* us, and as Itself *in support of us*. We are "His" evolution, as "He" is ours. So, when you get your mind wrapped around this constant cycle you are in, you can see that it is not a question of *lacking* power at all, but of being so caught up in *redundant application of mind* that we are essentially asleep. We have got ourselves so well self-mesmerized, we scarcely miss a beat!

It does no good to talk of political promises and future possibilities if, as individuals, we cannot get ourselves to stand up on our own two feet. We hesitate upon the brink of something wonderful, doubtful of ourselves for breaking rank with idiots -- maybe they are right and we are wrong, after all! -- and then it's back to the same old repetitions more acceptable. The problem isn't all the nonsense they get up to in the Capitol. It isn't the job; it isn't the wife; it isn't the pancreas, or the mothballs in the billfold. If we are stumbling forward with a half-forgotten dream that won't unfold, it can only mean that we are thinking much the same as we have always done; that we are giving too much credence to the reruns of our eyeballs. It's a safer bet, you see, than turning around to face the "certainty" of ... *evil.*

It comes down to nitpicking at ourselves over questions of integrity; often not willing to face some bitter truth about ourselves, tossing the unacknowledged trouble away from conscious view where it seems to apply more conveniently to someone else; and then we are caught in a loop of pain and blame, admitting little or nothing to our immaculate selves. So there tends to be a chronic condemnation of ourselves, subliminally, that underpaints our rosy points of view, and this effectively blocks and erodes our sense of power with a range of uncomfortable emotions we don't want to get into. This dynamic is kept in place by long tradition of science and religion -- which are, afterall, systems of belief of *individuals.* Our power lies in the actual operating current of the Stream of consciousness we flow, which science denies and religion essentially forbids; and though we are only talking, at electro-chemical levels (once imbibed), of mere millivolts, that is the current of our lives. "Above" and "below" the thresholds of our wakeful thinking are many other strata of mind, and we are more active at other levels than we suppose. But root assumptions about the nature of reality, that amount to rigid dogmas and patterns of avoidance (religious, scientific, philosophical, moralistic, metaphysical), have so long entrained us to an under-educated syllopsis (to coin a new word) of lopsided thought, we actually imagine ourselves to be disconnected from *everything!* If hell or magma or primate tendencies wait "below", and Judgement or smarter humanoids or interstellar cold being sucked into black holes "above", it is no wonder to me that we hide out this side of "unconscious" and busy ourselves in our redundancies. But it does not serve us well in the long haul of escaping from these mental cages.

"Sovereignty" is a legal term for the substantive basis of a very real power in our lives -- that of Source or consciousness-flow itself ("God" considered only in terms of an available presence of force, which is surely not the whole picture by a long shot) -- which we are ill-equipped to speculate coherently about without a sacred science of mind, even though we exercise ourselves in mode of concentration all the time. Here, I am only pointing up the complications that arise, and will arise more prevalently, when questions of individual sovereignty, in human rights and group self-governance, come more into active play between stewards and citizens and the various echelons of church, corporate, and state. At present, sovereignty tends to be seen as something handed down from higher authority, or else so spread out in the populace at large in a soupy porridge of a concept that it has no practical relevance but in a paltry vote. The danger in this should be obvious: those "inalienable rights" inherent in human nature seem reduced to paper privileges handed down from on high. We entrust too much to those with the burden and license to be our representatives. A privilege is not a right. A vote is not self-governance.

Sovereignty, then, currently locked up in issues of authority (and utterly irrelevant in the domains of science), is released in explorations of *selfhood*. But the prevalent notion of selfhood is essentially an amputation of head and foot: it is seen purely as egohood and physicality -- a stance in material reality only, without source or purpose, without interior range and recourse to a wealth of intelligent aid. This is a dangerous frame of mind -- and virtually all of our private and social ills trace back to it: to an isolated, hardened egohood in tenuous defense against environment. Life is crudely regarded in terms of "survival of the fittest" in a predatory state -- even *economics* is so perverted! All evidence of the cooperative basis of nature -- without which nature would not even be possible! -- is severely twisted and misunderstood by a deeply ingrained delusion and education solely obsessed with ego experience. Our public schools are crippling, not enlightening, minds. This can only have disastrous consequences unless it is broadly understood that "self" is more than simply looking outward; and that such ego orientation under constant stress eventually implodes. It needs to be assured of, through its interaction with, the constant supports available to it from other strata of mind, some levels of which are evidently more sensitive to the whole workings of the surround, the realm of the ministers and adjutants of ... *Deity*.


II.


Behavioral psychology bumbles around creating untold mischief in unwittingly sitting on heads to squish the psyche down to something thin and utterly seethrough, like a handkerchief; they fold it over once or twice to give it layers for sifting through, but basically it's just a cushion for a butt to sit. But lest you think I'm being too hard on your therapist, I hasten to add that we are all self-psychologists in that we contemplate ourselves, our psyches, and tend to reduce the Mystery of Selfhood to mere egohood and one or two psychoses. Basically, we are sitting on our own heads. It's cheaper that way. We share in common a model of the psyche that is basically three pancakes thick: with a "conscious" mind on top, getting all the syrup and butter; under this, a "subconscious" layer of dubious reputation; and under that, an "unconscious" layer that is apparently downright evil. "Soul" doesn't really fit this picture, in professional circles, so we tend to throw it out as completely irrelevant; and if we must include an overseeing God, make it one big mouth about to take a bite, or a salivating appetite just sniffing us out, wondering if there are any blueberries. But since consciousness by *any* name is just the smoke of this, according to authorities, consensus is that *none* of this is real, and therefore "self" is just an accidental *body* with an incidental fate, and we are only contemplating, more or less, nothing but a sticky plate.

But then we wake up some early morning out-of-body, wondering at the stranger in our bed (beside the wife!), and then we're back to pancake-flipping, trying to reason out the proper height of mental states stacked up in a heap to explain an impossible life. By rights, we should be dead, if, as they say, "we are what we *think* we are," yet *thought* does not exist! There is something psychotically mad and dangerous to psychological health in all this science ignoring the very consciousness it reasons with. Psychology tries to bridge the gap between the ego's frustrated behavior and its Pavlovian morals, but all its bridging reaches out to nowhere. In science general, hypotheses collapse with every new subatomic dot theoretically "proved" and then conveniently "discovered" (more or less) -- they're basically down to a massless mass, and thoroughly confused as to what is holding all this nothingness together. (*Perception*, of course, but since it's too confounding to their differential math, particles of mass must infinitely reduce down to their source in ... you guessed it ... other dots.) All in all, a Catholic mass seems less unfortunate.

It's rather like picking one's own pocket, isn't it? A kind of lopsided wealth: one side keeps disappearing, while the other side is amassing bits. And it all looks *awfully familiar*. I guess discordant halves of mind need *something* to do. And there's no denying that science has figured something out, for look at all the gadgets! Now we can meet in chat rooms without having to look at each other! We can listen to the news instead of getting hit with it! We can do more things while driving, when all you could do on a horse was sit! You can learn all there is to know about the mechanics of life from a little mechanical frog, all you have to do is kill it. There's no denying it: science has a brilliant mind for making clever widgets; and *life-saving* devices too, let's not forget: now we can get in even more overtime, and we don't even have to be conscious.

Don't get me wrong, technology is one of the great wonders of the world. It's just the difficulty of living with it.

Science and technology have their uses. Preempting strata of mind with bipolar circuitry is not one of them. Our spirituality has not kept up with it. We are *far* more rich in breadth and scope of multidimensional mind and personhood than is generally supposed. It only takes a mild curiosity and gentle probing of one's own subjective states to find out where our temporal and spatial boundaries are -- beyond those, a further range, other probabilities, other frameworks of reality in which we also go exploring, and find ourselves with other names. The ego, looking down its nose upon a "solid" landscape, preoccupied with daily affairs, barely gives a backward glance toward the deeper states from which it rises every morning, to which it sinks in guilty pleasure every evening. Throughout the night, the body does its best to regenerate in maintenance mode, while the mind goes on minding. Outer ego becomes inner ego; reality shifts from solid-state to semi-solid, to absolutely manifold; from frozen concentrate to real fruit on the bough; from a self-hypnotic state, through entertaining veils of self-delusion, into ever more increasingly lucid states. Basically, the ego's world is a closet, in comparison to the mansion worlds of the whole self, which only wears its sparkling ego like a diamond; but the mind is full of diamonds.

I suppose this basic duality that so engages and entrains us -- the good and evil of morality, the positive and negative poles of energy -- comes of being ourselves of a dual nature: from broad perspective to narrow perspective, we expand

and contract ourselves like rubber bands; soul and ego somewhat outrageously mismatched in a cosmic dance that has the one head reeling around the room, the other planted firmly center of the universe like an Easter Island head -- a monolithic mystery looking up at who knows who. Ego perspective says: this little thing "I am" is all I own; circumscribed by a dubious and uncertain view; beyond that, oblivion. Soul perspective says: this grand and glorious entity "I am" describes a circle big enough for point of view of me *and* you, like two eyes on a single head; like two "I's" in a single cranium, with two hemispheres of a brain in one all-encompassing heaven.

The thing about a closet is: no one ever puts a window in. It's just a place for hanging up our attitudes.

There seems to be a basic insecurity in present human nature, like a spinning top that wobbles uncertainly on a taut string stretched between the two ends of our identity. We do our best to hide this fact, to appear secure whilst we cling to home or mate or office, or *anything* that seems to offer safe harbor from the infinite sea of untried possibilities. There is strength also; self-confidence, self-esteem, self-trust; a bubbling up of boundless curiosities; the glimmer of inspiration from a wiser if enigmatic dream. Environment acts like a mirror sometimes, reflecting back upon us some synchronicity that shows us to ourselves, what we thought we held tightly under lid of secrecy, brewing up a new event. The genesis of new sensitivities has us crowing up the soul one moment, whimpering from "abandoned" egohood the next. All this coming and going between inner and outer realities has us spinning around in a revolving door; it's difficult to get our bearings: Am I a giant or a midget? Am I a god or a bore? But all judgments and definitions and condemnations aside, the one glaring fact is: I am I. And without all the names and labels and limits put to this, a "self" is just another kind of globe or particle, in another kind of orbit, in another kind of infinite. So who is there so infinitely wise to

91

explain to me what it is that I can and cannot do? What it is that I can and cannot think and feel and have and dream and be? Sometimes I feel like a hardboiled egg bouncing around in a boiling pot, all arrogancy and insecurity wrapped up in a cracking shell of isolated egohood. But I swear to you, I am going to blow the lid off this: I am going to make a deviled egg of me.

Historically, the leading edge of thought has always moved around a bit. A new idea takes hold of inquisitive minds, and suddenly semi-naked natives are mapping the heavens and building pyramids in the middle of a jungle or a desert; hackers of heads are building empires out of brick and bone and blood and mortar; knights and troubadours are galavanting around the countryside in noble quest of higher order; monks and rabbis at their chemistry sets are counting bumps on heads, or clumps of angels or elements or lumps and beads and threads of *anything* that adds up to a quantifiable intelligence. Civilizations come and go like stubborn fads. The divine right of kings and queens and popes and all robes laureate are basically a fashion show: they went out with a "told you so." Peasants basically run the show now, or just now figuring out they always did. Once upon a time, long, long ago, I think we must have lived upon the world as in a dream, and history is the fleshing-out of painted strokes, for we are still world-making, and this morning's episode still has the ancient scent of something wet as Borneo or Mesopotamia; something Chinese even here in Idaho; there are fingerprints on everything; the dream itself is biting at its fingernails and thinking, thinking.

The latest scope of our surveillance has us thinking about our thinking itself. All this thinking, all this scope, all this messing around inside and all around ourselves, and still the masterpiece is dripping ink of possibilities too wildly entertaining to contain ourselves. Frame on frame of canvas at every blinking: we are too perfectionist; we are dissatisfied with everything; we are Leonardos, two-fisted, double-lobed, de

Vincing everything; up to our elbows in lead of pencil-dust and still we are redesigning; up to our eyeballs in blueprints and models. We are addicted to everything, but we are honest squires; it is not enough anymore to have our powers up in heaven, or down in subterranean holes: we are playing at being gods ourselves, painting our own exaggerated faces on the domes of one anothers' craniums; the brain is a lightning storm of electrical agitations, and somewhere in our own cave-shadows we are looking at how to find ourselves in these cathedral ceilings, summoning angels out of heaven to feed us grapes. We have more or less figured out that we are more than just our primate bodies. We have forgotten some things in adding more to our estates; but we are re-remembering, little by little, where we lost or last hid old articles of ourselves in treasuring after new ideas and things. This is my grandiloquent way of explaining how we have come to be such bold little cowards, caught like flies in the webs of our own spiders: thinkers of realities, dripping in showers -- what a mess we make of thinking. What a show of psychic flowers.

We tend to think of our ancestors, Ug and Lee, as ignorant cavemen dragging their women about by the hair; then wonder at the delicate beads in their braids, and what their talismans must have said, whispering in the shadows of the shadows. We do not see the Paleolithic intent of our own crude instruments, digging up their sacraments, taking careful measurements of their opened graves, counting their excellent teeth. They couldn't put a man on the moon, so they brought the planets down to earth, and we are still trying to figure out the math. Those rich minds of imaginative and intuitive and emotional range and worth, that could still learn from animals and talk to trees and conjure information out of Mother Earth, and bring down a Father's rains by stomping on his dirt, and send the gods back wiser than they came, licking their self-inflicted hurts: I think our ancestors would think it plumb silly of us that we are so proud of our newfound intellectual

93

prowess counting beans, when there are so many mouths to be fed, and maidens to be brought up right and wed, and sons to be taught how to make a bed, and proud chiefs taught how to bow the head. I think they knew how to dream with intent, and how to come and go from a vision of things; how to launch a thought and follow after it; how to communicate from eyes and lips alike, by genuinely *meaning* it; how to follow a stream by leaning into a gleam of light or gazing upon a moving reflection: the head was not then a cage of restricted selfhood, but a nest of open-ended thoughts into which tribes of Sun and Moon and far off Star dropped feathered messages down to adorn the head. There were books before there were alphabets, but it took an open mind to read such genesis seeding ideas sprouting tangible out of every cranny and nook. Yes, I think they would laugh at us, at all our seriousness after gadgetry, mourning our own forgetfulness of all self-meaning and all self-purpose in all this busyness of dream-making ... except, of course, that they are *Us:* it is hard to laugh at oneself after so many dusty leagues. Even so slight a passing shadow as death is taken seriously these days. We have not yet figured out, for all our calculus, how to measure the infinite worth of dust.

Life is the revelation of our own harmonics, yet science is still giving us particles galore. Consciousness, to these well-meaning but pretentious hacks, is something of a dead geranium; and nature is only a thing of parts, subject to the slow decay of uranium. All that lies outside one's bubble of thought is conceived as an external force -- one or another movement of electromagnetic radiation -- or just blandly tossed off as unknowable sea of dark; "collective unconscious", in the jargon of psychology. So says the unseeing shadow to the flame of its source, which it has not the wherewithal to see, as the eye cannot compute a brightness more radiant that its sun.

I would not be so quick to flee from warmth of Source just because I could not put it under thumb. Science is

94

unfortunately two-dimensional, and emotions are unquantifiable; but they are not unknowable, except to a frightened intellectualism afraid of its own guns. What we need is a science less addicted to the numbness of its numbers; that has an ear for music, and an eye for fun; curious minds not so damned afraid of studying dreams by actually having one, brave enough to cross a threshold without a calculator, to encounter one's other side in other terms than simple sums. Only then can we have a model of selfhood that actually informs us of who we are without the blindness of an infantile ego running in its one direction only. If consciousness can design a microscope, then it *is* one, and only needs to look back upon itself less afraid.

If we must think in terms of quantum particles, then these lifeless theoretical bits simply will not do. And wave theory does little better. These conceptual motes and squiggles are denied all reference to the innate consciousness that perceives and projects them. Give us a head of diamonds and rubies, for then we can at least get a sense of our dignity and worth; facets of selfhood in geometric relationship, a scope of knowing to go exploring in. Better yet, imagine a vast symphony thousands of instruments strong, in an orchestra pit as big as a stadium, yet so muted that we can only imagine it; and that is an image of a single electron --- the means by which we sing ourselves into being, string ourselves along, even enduring the percussion of our diseases; the brassy fanfare of self-applause -- stand up and take a bow for yourself for having the panache to think at all; the woodwinds of stirring up some feeling of romance; the strings of divine ambition, sublimest of all. Or, in terms of emotional coloration, which surely makes up a third of our intelligence at least, somewhere between the interrelation of this ethereal glow and diamond spectacle of our incarnation we are traveling back and forth across a quantum harmonic bridge, like angels in and out of heaven, coexisting in twin states, simultaneously sound-exploring and wobbling physical.

Orthodox science is a dead relative I never even liked; I will not even go to the funeral. What lives in me is full of life; I will not hear it otherwise. I will drink my fill of it, or live on fumes; I will not eat the stuff of tombs.

It is not that I see no value in scientific training and invention, but that I think its greatest value goes overlooked. Yes, the capacity for abstract thinking has a clear advantage over utter stupidity; idiocy invents nothing. And I, too, tend to share the scientist's general aversion to the airy-fairy romanticism and sentimentality of religious and spiritual vagueness and rigid morality. But the greater value of scientific training is not its end result of mechanical invention, practical and entertaining as these inventions quite often are; rather, to my way of thinking, an abstraction of thought is a *construct of consciousness* that (when consciousness itself is validated as something more than chemical farts) can therefore be utilized inwardly in much the same way as a physical structure is utilized outwardly. Abstract thinking contributes enormous content to other frameworks of reality, but who dares to cross over into one of these forbidden zones? This contribution to, and participation in, other frameworks of reality is the real discovery and "invention" here, more significant than mechanical invention, which ultimately but *mimics some capacity or other of the creative mind projecting design.* The capacity for multiplicitous experience in alternate versions of reality is the real frontier.

But ego-bound thinking studies everything from the *outside*, like a swimmer sticking his toe in the certainty of an ice-cold lake, and forty years later still cannot bring himself to take a dip. What is "reality", in quantum terms, but *probabilities* -- alternate versions of things and events: these, the *mind can lean into* where instruments cannot. The entire world, essentially, is just a grand and intricate *Idea* that unfolds before curiosity like a flower.

96

III.

Such existential probing always brings me back around to the subject of my own innate divinity, and I am reluctant to let the idea go to soothe the insecurities of a pack of skeptics. But "deity" is a disturbing topic to many people; to those who feel it their duty to cower under some engraven image of a bearded Zeus; and particularly to those who feel it their professional responsibility to refrain from asking a metaphysical question at all. Yet it is a legitimate question, and one not difficult at all to ponder: What is the nature of God? What is the meaning of "divinity"? What is my relation to this intriguing Mystery? More importantly, what would such an august Intelligence find so interesting about me, to make such provision for the rudiments of life as It so profusely does?

It is too easy for me to be contemptuous of unquestioning minds: the death of curiosity stinks. The smugness of undiscovered crime, the bludgeoning of young minds with blunt instruments of narrow "faith" and "logic", the political takeover and sterilization of the schools -- I've had to claw my way through the ranks of unenlightened leaders like everybody else. I observed a few rare souls, little giants, stand their ground against the bully tactics of "experts"; but mostly I observed the silencing of the lambs on graveyard playgrounds; souls more like embryos, who do as they are told because that is yet the extent of their range. What a monstrous length of time it takes to get the will to move an inch. But why do I pretend to be amazed at this? Consider the context of our upbringing, how one must start from the vulnerability of naked infancy to grow and develop one's weapon of choice against a designed hostility. So I will strive for more sympathy and understanding, more tolerance of old philosophies. I will pretend I do not see the slip showing. But do not hold your breath for me: there is still the burden of honesty.

97

There is no question in my mind but that life is designed. I find it embarrassing to think otherwise, an insult to basic intelligence. I will not ever be willfully blind for the sake of maintaining a thin film of prestige. Nor will I ever concede all creativity to an old tribal god, and ignore the obvious creativity bequeathed to me. As human beings, we are creators in our own right, and obviously share in this mystery of 'divinity" -- how has this utter simplicity escaped so many for so long? They must have been looking at their feet! Or maybe the struggle for survival and reputation -- some constant of stability or ... dare I say it?... *love* -- hijacks our attention, keeps us distracted all that way from the cradle to the grave; and it is only *afterward* that we think to question the reasons for such a predatory arrangement of things.

I mean, really, were dinosaurs necessary? Were flesh-eating animals? The planetary quarantine of humanity in a multiverse administration of foes? Because we were orphans, were we never entitled to more than scraps of information about our cosmic parents, and enigmatic revelations of our souls? There is no question in my mind but that life was designed ... but designed for what? And by whom?

I will give you my best-sounding answer, let it sink or float as it will -- I'll skip it to you like a flat, round stone: I think life on Earth was designed to foster *faith*. I don't mean "faith" in the credal sense, as a euphemism for a set of beliefs; but faith as a reliance upon unseen supports. Hell, any old school can teach the basics of getting along together like good boys and girls. It takes a *predatory* world, where supper is always in question, boom or bust, to create a strong and independent mind. And nothing can move the proverbial mountain, against all odds, like a terrible force of *trust.*

On Earth, we put our faith in whom we know not; there is a confusion of possibilities. We *have* to, just to get through a day; and we do it whether we realize it or not. Even the atheist, poor befuddled fellow, *trusts* his way through the daily obstacles, *hoping* against a run of zero luck. Don't tell that to him; he will argue himself insensible. Like the capacity for logic, or morals, we have an innate capacity to venerate the Invisible, innately bridging ourselves to the whole mysterium that has its army encamped around our walls and tapping a metallic finger at the gate.

## IV.

As science must eventually come to terms with the power of its Sun, the engine that drives everything in the context of physicality; and as religion must eventually come to terms with the presence of *its* Son, as the driving power of curiosity; so must we all, in our own peculiar combinations of logic and faith, come to amicable terms with the One who so saturates our every particle and chemical bond that there is no existing separately.

But herein lies a profound and disturbing problem: for science and religion both presume to have shot that One dead with the selfsame gun.

Certain casualties are to be expected, of course, in the dog-eat-dog climate of speculation and respectability. I am in agreement with science that all tribal deities had to go. Men do not progress well in fear of their alternatives: they must *love* their Unknown. But the arrogance of presuming to deprive a mind of its subjective Source in *intelligence*, to dismiss us all as an accidental burp of primordial soup is, forgive me, a joke. Considering "God" in its broadest context, as that which initiates and holds all rounded things in their mysterious and inexplicable orbits, All That Is could hardly be dead. Only scientific hope, evidently. Still all nuclei adhere to their closets; nothing has come unglued. And the great intelligences who oversee the administration of these far-flung evolutionary worlds and morontia universities still are showing up, where invited, in intuitional instruction and unfathomable dreams. Clearly, relativity and quantum arithmetic do not explain everything.

Religion, for its part, is an equally bumbling assassin. I am in agreement with every village dope, who looks around in glass-eyed amazement at the obvious and sublime beauty of divine attainment, rightly concludes a Fire at the source of all shapes and sizes of material smoke, and *feels the purpose of things,* and the *irresistible pull of Source.* His is the grandest of minds, which knows the Designing Mind as *his;* not *its.* Religionists have that much going for them at least, that whatever they lack in curiosity, they are generally not as enslaved to the humdrum of counting mathematical bits to build a universe out of Nothing. Every mosque, church, and temple knows the outsideness of things as the tabernacle, at least, of *that which presides within.* If they are more or less loathe to approach so luminous a Son, as science shrinks from the fusion-furnace of the source of all science in helium, it can hardly be counted against them I love to poke fun at our corious dogmas of sin and solar radiance, as if our mighty minds have spanned end-to-end the entire lengths of eternity and infinity, which *have no ends.* All our knowledge requires two bookends, for it never stands up under scrutiny.

But religion presumes to put a gun to the head of God in killing off every indication of emerging divinity. Enough of these superstitious ghost-fears and tribal servility. We act like our own bodies have been crucified, not just our possibilities. We are too compliant, torn between loyalties to a Fatherly Soul extremely difficult for us to comprehend, and the traditional tribal deity who otherwise stands in. It is no wonder that we are yet stooges to nanny government and petty economic servitudes: we are still trying to appease Authority that we cannot comprehend, instead of noticing that we are *being it*. Our religions are becoming a social embarrassment; why so few attend. And the new priesthoods of science are already derailing the cars up ahead, a snake with no sensitive tongue, and shedding its aluminum skin, still pushing from behind like a candy-greedy fat-boy on the scent of free samples. A cold-hearted calculus driving industry, be forewarned, is a hazard on too many wheels. The profit motive of industry is not an end in itself, if anyone cares to notice; but the typical worker/consumer is far too servile and compliant and complicit to help matters. There is no backbone, no spiritual confidence, no recognition of sonship for the poor orphaned kids. Humanity is climbing it ideals to a high concept of Earth Prime, but Christ was put down as a lame duck idea, and the climb has since been slippy-platypus. Which is to say, that as long as "sonship" hangs crucified in the back of our minds, our own spiritual life is effectively blocked; and we will continue to live and die as mice.

What a barbarous idea that salvation from "sin" requires a blood sacrifice to appease an angry god. Who stands under such sentence but a child of voodoo in naked ignorance of its own parentage. Such theology is born in villages with too many hacked-off limbs; from children early accustomed to traumas, the discipline of the macheté, growing up into priesthoods and universities, an insatiable appetite for validation and money. "Christ and him crucified," that old symbol of our own mourning, barely conceals our war memories, when we yearned for a motherly or fatherly touch, from Whom we knew not; *air* as far as one could conjure at a moment's warning. Angry parents and disapproving looks are the education of humanity, and now the driving gears of insatiable industry.

Where is God but in a book, to a maimed child grown haphazardly, barely motivated to read the stupid thing.

The slow ascent from servitude to sonship, from potenti- ality to actuality, from democracy to confidence; the expansion of our sensorium that begins with the real recognition of Fatherhood, to appreciation of our *own* sonship, to the brotherhood experiments of something colonial and daring: such dreams are not something so easily achieved by those who still so arduously resist the first green impulses of their own divinity. Every hole in the earth is the bite of a snake to those who live barefoot by the stinking riverbank of some social current after cheap refugees. It is a grand leap from this to a clean realization of transcendent inheritance. It is a tough haul, but I will see what I can do to see you over this dirty ditch.

*"Of all the things that men have come to fear:*
*The fear of God; the fear of hell; the fear of death;*
*The greatest fear of all would seem to be*
*The fear of Self."*

**Cantos from the Ghost of Lincoln.**

*"Still we have in our midst, as in our outlying colonies, those small cliques of well-meaning but rather trying people who have great difficulty even in the modern age accepting anything constructed of atomic material beyond their tactile sensory range. Only yesterday I met with a colleague of mine from 608, whose temporal charge is a renowned scientist of his world, a member of a very prestigious research firm, still working within the parameters of only 98 or so of the heavy atomic elements. The full spectral duplicates of these elements are still something of an incredulous mystery. They understand the concept of isotopes, and ionic coupling, but nothing of the adjustable space of the closure around the nuclei, so the lighter doubles of their visible elements remain largely outside of the purview of their reality-domain. You and I could be standing right in front of them, and some of them would not even see us. They would think us quite unreal without the aid of their more perceptive fellows, and even then would be stubbornly skeptical."*

> Astari Manuscript, Book III,
> *Astronautical Summary of the Tripartisan Arena*.

\* \* \* \* \* \* \*

Essay 5:

## The Force That Guides The Flower.

I.

What a peculiar type of man is this "steward" I dream of: an individualist in the extreme, almost to the exclusion of having friends; for how could one walk such a fine line and still socialize with idiots? The ways of modern man, so animal and communal, so conformist and afraid, would seem to *do him in,* for what has a steward to do with those who *huddle:* he listens to some voice within; he does not "fit in"; he lives by principle, which is a threat to even his nearest of kin, who live by gossip

107

and complaint, by ostentation and by spectacle -- but only to the limits of their chains.  He is out of rank and out of uniform, is our little steward; thinks he's some kind of knight or troubadour, without a horse, without a sword, without a date; he acts as if he's been initiated, knows something more than what they teach at university.  He is breaking the rules of the game, and scaring us all with talk of "sovereign immunity."  There is talk of lynching him, or shaving his head when he sleeps -- *anything* to make him open up, and tell us why he's so determined to upset everyone and everything, and then we fear we'll not be strong enough to shut him up.

Then in the same breath to talk of "tribal sovereignty" ... I must need my head examined, for how can such as these who do not clump up even *find each other*, let alone establish in the midst of us a *colony*?  When the standard forty-hour work-week is the law of God; a house and picket fence owned by the bank, the dream of dreams; when an individual's credit rating is the way we keep score; our cars are duly registered; we only buy a lottery ticket, honest, once a week; and listen to the latest president's State of the Union speech every year, like clockwork; half, at least, depending how it interferes with other program-ming.  (He is really doing something this year, so they say.  I haven't really noticed.)  With all of these clear evidences of our social ease, our camaraderie, our well-oiled political and social machinery, why upset ourselves with the niceties of all this so-called "public stewardship"; of social responsibilities?  We have our damned communities, is that not enough?

Far be it from me to disagree.  It's all I can do myself to wake up.  I try to live like a steward, a man of spine, with a vision of things, a code of honor.  I feel for the people of the street, but I seldom succomb and give a dollar:  it does not empower neediness to fill a hole that will only open back up in an hour.  If they asked for a *kingdom* instead, I'd offer them a glimpse of spacious possibilities.  But they don't look like they'd be very interested. I don't think they know what they want. A bed? A shower? They have had these once; and we all know already what it is to sleep and be clean, and be ready for another day of chasing after another dollar. Yet I am also prone to walking away from meaningless labor that is only paying someone else's mortgage, so I am myself quite often in need of a stack of dollars. I write for money; I write for pleasure. Nothing at all is changing around me as a result of this; except, of course, that *everything is.*

For all my resounding and convoluted words, I cannot lift one thought of yours above the mean, the average, the high-water mark that you have so well established for yourself, or denied yourself. I can only throw a profusion of sounds, because it delights me to do so; a stimulation of things suggestive of shapes in a cloud, and whatever you can make of these. It makes nothing happen, of course; a cloud remains a cloud. For all my philosophical posturing, a crowd remains a crowd. Still, I am looking forward to my book. It is its own happening. I want to see my words filling page after page, and hold in my hands the box of gems that is the reward for all my years of hard-earned thought. All my readers but look on; some are amazed, some are not; one or two are moved sometimes to an occasional sentimental tear; another will tell me he received nothing more from me than a paper cut. Some doors are open; some doors are shut. But me, my eyes are open, and by sharing what I see there is implied an opportunity and an invitation for you to see the same, or something of that vista if you will take a look.

For some, the kingdom of heaven is in a mustard seed; or an embryonic soul in a social knot. Some will computate a quantum dot, and calculate the speed it takes to jump on top. For others, longing remains on the simple order of a shower, a can of beans, and a sleeping cot, until the hour comes when it does not.

109

Consider for a moment the mansion worlds that lie all about you on another plane of thought. The kingdom of heaven is far, far away for those who are living what they are living that throws God out of orbit at such high velocity. Yet they will all go dutifully to church in the morning, you can bet your holy socks. They will sing the same praises to whom they know not; and kneel when they are told, even if their knees do not quite agree with them. They will turn to page such-and-such, trying their bestest to hurry up; consider every point given, turned over and over for them like an omelette with a gold-plated spatula, in no need whatsoever of any real disagreement. "The kingdom of heaven is within you," they will read, again; and again not hear it. They will yearn for more than they can see; and seeing, not know it. They will plead for more than they can hear; and listening, not believe it. For it is not yet in them to feel any one of the mansion worlds so close at hand. It is in them to fear it.

It is not entirely in me either to discern these layered worlds of reality. I but dream it will be possible at any minute. I try to imagine having an eye that can see, and an ear that can hear. Damn it! I am no better than any one of these smug believers in demons and feeders of fears. I want, but I cannot bring myself to get comfortably near them; they repel nonbelievers with *talking* of love, but they feed only old fish on a spear.

We are too much alike for sincere kidding, humanity and I. Too many vulgarize everything. Others say the same of me, can you believe it. Earth Prime, in contrast to this -- as a broader version of the world accessible to anyone who achieves some degree of proficiency in perceiving it -- is a far cry closer than I mean to hurl it.

But if this ideal is all we've got, let us make the most of it. To actually know God as a Father, I find, is not such an easy leap as so many pretend. They are being obedient is all; and

110

obeisance is not free and clear. They are saying words like "Love" and "Spirit," and steering clear of words like "Judge" and "Tyrant," but their meaning is clear enough in acting so mulish: they are feeling plugged in the chest by a plague of locusts and panics. Life is, for many, a test; a drug; a labyrinth of meat-eaters: "He never answers a prayer!" "I'm talking to the ceiling!" "I'm talking to the air!" There must be something more to this than even our revered leaders have any real inkling for hearing or seeing. We are all kidding ourselves: we are usually looking at something else.

We are looking at ourselves in each others' mirrors, but not seeing gods. We are seeing smears. We are feeling embarrassed to be ourselves. We are sucking-in the gut and looking for honesty in beauty or muscle. But the life of the soul is the farthest reflection in our minds. Whatever the interior of ourselves might be thinking, down there in its own domain, is something we do not usually consider. It is the orphan boy we keep barely alive in its cupboard under the stairs. Point to yourself: we invariably locate the "I am" in its seat in the chest; the "soul's seat." So who is this clowning around in our heads? An interesting point to put somewhere.

Some part of us lives in an embryonic state; is not having much, if anything at all, to do with our social affairs. This is our "safe deposit box," and how we live in relation to it determines our wealth.

II.

To say that the soul is embryonic is really something of a misnomer. What is embryonic is our *sense* of ourselves. We are the long shadows cast in the soulful eclipse of our primary Blaze. It is equally true to say that the body is safely ensconced in its "spirit;" that we are well-cocooned in broader identities, looking in on ourselves from beyond our imaginings, and looking out from within our closets. The words we use to delineate different parts of our subjective experiences -- "ego," "soul," "spirit" -- suggest separations that do not exist in the actual continuum of our being, being so multipli-focused in our "house of mirrors" ... we are just not mature enough in our psychological range to venture "out" into wherever we happen to be focused "in" it. We are too particular, and thus too particulate: our familiarity with things does not generally extend very far beyond the limits of the visible light spectrum, which focalizes, and thus singularizes, infinity into single images and digits. When something moves without visible means, we usually take fright and show our tribal origins. Yet our very brains function variously at different speeds -- at infrared, at ultraviolet, in microwaves, many octaves -- so we are more actively engaged in a consortium of alternative selves than we're able to believe. Because we are more or less babes, it seldom occurs to us how quickly our minds are actually *selving*, replicating like cells. We think we have figured out just about everything worth scoping, yet even as adults it is hard to resist putting things in our mouths. But as a toddler will crawl from room to room to new wonderments, so do the mansion worlds await the scaling effect of multisensory curiosity, when the mind grows out of its protective arrogance.

As our biological cells must replicate through nucleonic cell-division to keep us physically alive, so do the "mota" of our minds. (I will explain this in just a moment.) But mentation is no mere house of mirrors, for we are trafficking in consciousness at multiple frequencies: we are out ahead of ourselves, and dragging behind, simultaneously experiencing events in different schematics of "time," of "environment," of "universe." That is, we are living simultaneous lives, and replicating whole worlds accidentally on purpose.

So, when the yeast is in the dough, which part is ego and which part is soul?

Even biologically we are composed of electron *orbits*: we are pluralistically composed, but knowing ourselves as a singularity. We are "black holes" in the greater cosmos of ourselves, sucking on everything; and "white holes" spewing starlight and solar energy, whole registries of intermediates in ministry, doting on ourselves, condensing superconsciousness into baby particles, because that's all we can yet eat of it. But mind also grows, through *mota* development; and spiritual polarity, creating morontia duplicates that guarantee, for now, our mortal longevity; later, our immortality.

In the broader scheme of things, life in the field is only a minor inconvenience, and death is but a short holiday; then it's back to the old routine of practice and study in the endless chain of multiversities.

For "now," given our chosen "locality," we are still generally passive perceivers: we take in the all-surround more or less ignorant of the exteriorization of ourselves. But remember, *perception is everything*, and anything perceived is more or less an extension of the perceiver. As this becomes more consciously *held*, perception becomes more active: the brain's sensorium develops more aggressively, as the "soul's" underlying super-sensitivity begins to *overlay* the "ego's" undersensitivity; and the mass-projected world of Idea-tangibility takes on more dimension and less density. The mid-conscious realm of our current predicament, acclimating to itself as such, bridges across the old ignorance of our pre-morontia selves, and matter itself replicates at double the order, so that our own senses, more developed, can examine all of this and satisfy its curiosity, as proof to itself, that self is indeed still godly and infinite, even in the midst of its specificities.

We need a new terminology for the realms ahead, and that's why I'm throwing in borrowed words like "mota" and "morontia" and "Mansonia," to stimulate curiosity. The soul that we are is even now perceiving, and knowing the all-surround differently; and you yourself have probably had enough experience by now to catch at least a glimpse of this, or it's unlikely you'd be reading this book. We are not bound to a five-sense world, a nickel-part stupid to a ninety-five-part sensitivity. Physicalized experience has its valued and intrinsic purposes. Certain things can be learned and designed in no other way. But we are evolving beyond our primary days; beyond our secondary days. A new genesis is pushing up new green in our understandings; the same force that guides the flower. Our sense organs variously translate certain quantum frequency fields into sense data, but our sensitivity is an evolving matter, and *has never been limited* to the cellular grapes and ganglion of our "translator devices" -- of ears, eyes, nose and tongue, and how these help us *touch* the idea-projections of our attached environs. We have greater sensory *capacity*, even now utilized "beneath our notice," whether we choose to sensitize ourselves to a further range or not. Otherwise, we are just addicted to our theories. It would be holo-grammatically incorrect to think otherwise; but I don't think anyone is really bothered.

"Mota" is a phenomenon that occurs with integrative thinking. It is entirely a *mental* organization (not specifically neurological), involving "thought packets" in a way, but can only *somewhat* be compared to cellular replication. Morontia substance and biological matter do not behave in exactly the same fashion. ("Morontia," remember, refers to the moral-ontological region of higher consciousness -- the mid-mind -- *between* the material and the spiritual.) Think of the interference patterns in a holographic plate, or interacting wavelets on a pond, all information-carrying: that is mota, direct perception or supersensitivity to what *is* -- all variables, all versions -- a

114

unifying perception of probabilities over and above what is logically deduced or faithfully believed based on sensory limits. Even the obvious "facts" of observation and direct revelation must be *interpreted.* Mota is how the soul perceives, superimposing its broader, direct perception over ego derivatives of narrowed faith and logic. Short of mota, *intuition* is the brain's best modem for reconciling conceptual differences.

"Earth Prime" is the dream of every secondary citizen: a world made green and alive again, shaking off the cough of a morning repetition. But the phlegm of faith and the ache of logic -- the perpetual war between the two hemispheres of the brain, of the heavens, of a congress; the bipolar domain of predatory industry and economics -- these split everything into left and right; into liberal and conservative, and two kinds of moderate; into irreconcilable differences between arrogance and stubbornness; between man and woman; between vanity and mirror. "God" lays waste "God" when he cannot integrate his feminine. And individuals grow cranky reading the same damn Book over and over. Yet it only takes a stretch of thought to overturn all argumentative things; to find one's strength again in conciliation of one's own good and better, and all polar opposites. The space between the electron cloud and the nucleus of every particle of our best perceiving bares a striking similarity to the space between our higher and lower logic; between hope and dead certainty in matters of faith; between the struggles of time and the velocity of dying. The mid-conscious realm has its own gravity, its own body, its own quantum material. And we are only reinventing our civilizations along the same lines because we're still dreaming.

When the eyes truly open, and stay open, it is a *steward* who awakens, and the Earth comes out of its morning delirium.

115

III.

In the absence of mota we have only the atomic: the continual effort to balance extremes: between positive and negative poles of force in our physics; between right and wrong choices in our psychic corral of black and white horses and rodeo clowns; between liberal and conservative loyalties, for those who want it straight. And to the extent that "we are only human," we have no choice but the limited range of our working material: *a hundred chemical elements* laid out on the periodic table, give or take a few, and whatever these little guys assemble into. The ethereal haze of electron cloud is basically the cage of our current delirium. We are Earth-bound. We are dirt-ridden. Electron activity defines the only "world" in which we seem to live, the electrochemical. Rarely does one glimpse any evidential other. The morontia material, on the other hand, after the grave in most cases, is at best but a secondary climate to us now. Few are looking down that well. That would take us down to heaven -- down into the truth of ourselves -- and that might prove to be a little hellish. For now, we have all the time and all the space of our science and our religion, the ups and downs of faith and logic on seesaws hammered out on every school playground. We have the arts, a merry-go-round on which to express our preferences; and monkey-bars for hanging upside-down and looking at the world different, or for showing off, swinging back and forth like a hairy congress.

Fortunately, we are *not* "only human," for there operates in us the fiduciary powers of innate knowing that would seem to be a gift from heaven. I mentioned these before as the built-in impulses of *curiosity*, *morality*, and *adoration*. This not only gives us, in general, our propensity for institutions of religion and science, but in our private minds the ever-shifting moral dilemmas between our curiosities and fascinations. What we worship, or fixate upon, or hold in awe, whatever commands our devotion, this matures in time, as we sift through the details of our experiences, distilling the pearls of wisdom from the meatiness of our discarded "crimes;" slowly evolving sensitivities from the cruelties of our intentions. We are still largely needy and manipulative creatures by the time we are adults, ever finagling for another's attention, not so willing to give it outright. But we are still *ascendant* creatures: little by little we become more sensitive, as a better alternative to being knocked senseless.

No one is ever more logical than his own logician, or ever more right than his own obvious. It is embarrassing to be caught stupid, so we cling to our diputs; like being raised up mightily in the big blue air on a seesaw when the other guy at the low end of the scale suddenly bails: he's got no argument, and he knows it, so he's out of it; but now you're left self-employed without a backup plan, without a parachute, and nothing to fall back on but your eminence. Any one of us can lecture another all day long on any point of evidence, it still comes down to the sole discretion of the other's solitaire and lonely decision. We can storm the castle, but never tradition: the citadel of the will has no rampart or gate, no way to invade the sovereign immaterial opinion of one who secretly weighs his own left and right, the moral juxtaposition between his most driving curiosity and insatiable appetite. Whether one venerates an ideal or an object, and reasons from a premise of obstinance or logic, the fulcrum of morality pivots on the razor's edge of self-determination, be he a hundred and seventy years old or seven; and a sovereign is a sovereign who not only holds his own stubborn head, but his own heaven. Only time and tide can educate one better-wise.

I understand the need for broad tolerance and long patience in waiting for the little guy to catch up with brilliance; that I myself have no right and no business -- and, indeed, no method, no real means -- to fault one who is only in heady pursuit of his own judgment or his own excitement; that the highest court of the land is not an institution, but the prick of conscience -- and that is a cactus that thrives on very little, grows only slowly, and in ever shifting sands. I also understand that cacti and mushroom, no different than flowers, have the inalienable right to congregate with their chosen fellows, and follow the revelations revealed by their most revered elders. I understand, I think, the sanctity of a saint, of an innermost cubicle or cupboard, of a venerable Book that is not of my booking, or of my race, or of my particular pinnacle; that even a weed grows in its own sacred space, by the mere fact that it *does* grow, and probably renders me some kind of medicine that I won't ever take. These things I understand, as the give-and-take between individuals serving out the terms of their preferences and agreements. We are the true stones of our civilizations, the mortar of our unions: the stubborn mules and pullers of our moving forward.

But it is another matter entirely when private preferments and groupings result in public executions, jihads, and inquisitions; or when public opinion and education are poisoned by the slow, insidious effects of a sterilized scientific indoc-trination. Blind devotion and narrow logic are fine things, I guess, in the pleasant company of their own admirings; but when such stagnancy turns so foul as to poison our very oxygen, then we have not just a private pleasing, but a cultural epidemic. The "antidote" is usually a revolution, bringing in another social order, yet more blood-letting and leeching and other antiquated teaching dusted off and brought forward. It gives the impression of a new house to rearrange the living room, but what it really indicates is a changing attitude. It's when we finally decide to be more honest with *ourselves,* or circumstances force us to, that private fixations and narrow logic broaden into bigger shoes that actually fit our bigger feet, and collectively our institutions remember how to advocate what they were created to: *the other man's religion,* and *the other man's logic:* for it is only our guarantee of another's *credence* that our own is secured. A lesson I find most troublesome.

In the final analysis, "civilization" is not the bully protection of the many against the most desperate and greedy; it is just the golden rule made more obvious.

Of course we have the right to question the wisdom of our institutions, in matters of faith, law and logic. And scientific dogma is as open to critical review as one-sidedness in religion. This is not to indict the individual believer or logician -- both of whom are more likely than not sitting in the same person -- nor is it to subpoena the institution, our friends and associates. It is when the organism as a whole suffers that we can no longer pretend justice; what we avoid comes looking for us with a vengeance; compels us to be more honest; and the crudities of our obsessions, and the blindness of avoidance, by and by accrue their daily due of remorse and repentance; we can always throw another tantrum, but after awhile even that ripens; wisdom eventually ensues, and soothes our complaints; sensitivity deepens; the world, to our slowly turning point of view, takes on a mysterious hue and coloration -- a moment of truth in a life of confusion -- and then comes the divine revelation: the "Truth" is only a fraction of the whole spectrum, and the spectrum is *forever.*

It takes an Observer to orchestrate a solid world out of frequency. It is just that science is afraid of itself: it knows its own tendencies. Religion likewise cowers under the mass projection of its own Image: chosen people are not insensitive to what they are capable of doing to the multitude of their exclusion. But as individuals, we are only *timid of the cosmos,* not intently criminal. Our hesitations and denials are only born of being skittish. *Invisibility itself* is the ghost that most frightens us, and not without reason. "God" is one name put to this; "Chaos" is another. Neither are very comprehensive

119

understandings; how can they be?  Without mota, we reason from the closure of our atoms.  They are the same, of course, an atom being the condensation and splitting of the whole-light spectrum into more specifics; like looking down the shaft of a telescope from the wrong end.  Mota, on the other hand, is a comprehensive sensitivity born out of the fusion of things reflected differently; it is looking down the shaft of a telescope from the right end, but looking at the astronomical proportions of ourselves spread out indifferently.  Mota is an integrative capacity of intelligence native to the soul -- the mid-mind -- available to anyone increasingly identified more with its wonderment than with its packaging.  The mota-atom inversion means:  we project what we are as our Reality; we *define* what we are by imaging.

An atom is a quantum package of light.  The Observer is the packager.  Mota is the reversal of light-perception from the density of heavy atomic to *spectral atomic* particles, for atoms are spectral:  they are differentials of frequencies; they are seven bodies in one, defined by the signatures of their orbitals, among other things.  And all things we know are composed of these, so we and all we know are seven stratums deep:  seven bodies in one, seven environments in one -- the mansion worlds.  A physically oriented mind can skate gracefully over these, with dark sunglasses on to cut the glare, making figure-eights on a frozen lake; it takes a deeper mind to perceive plumb.  But these are usually the deadbeats of the party.  We don't like to talk to those.  They probably don't even skate.  But any one of them will tell you, if you are secure enough in yourself and socially unafraid:  What a world will open up when you lose the shades.

Sensitivity is the *door,* and love the *key*, to an expanding sensorium that broadens the reality of one's perceptual range.  And because we are *projectors* of reality, in a *spectrum* of identity, the atomic world behaves according to dynamics that we ourselves impose, from concept to percept to down your

120

nose. We are ourselves the electron haze of our own Atom. We have only to soften the hard edges of our two extremes.

Religionist or scientist or any admixture in between, it behooves us as individuals to use *both* sides of our individuality … but to *use them both together*, not separately. As it takes two eyes together to perceive with depth the one solid environment, so faith and reason together in catalytic fusion will unlock the spectral elements of "heaven," the way a prism reveals in common daylight its composition out of Seven.

*"For in the dreams of such liberated littleness*
*Are sown the wild oats of Mind's*
*Utmost and limitless*
*Stars and greater Universities."*

**Cantos from the Ghost of Lincoln.**

*"Many a mystery would be solved with a basic understanding of the three gravities."*

Astari Manuscript, Book II,
*The Enigma of Reflectivity.*

*"Vast information is stored in a hydrogen bond, as is shared in the electron dynamics at the quantum level. Any kind of chemical bond implies an information-holding relationship. The ethereal elasticity of mental states (desires, intentions, fears), once compacted into supercharged molecular geometries, find excellent storage and conveyance in whole libraries of light-encoded proteins, hormones, and enzymes. Thus are the blueprints of consciousness stored in the crowded life plasm. And such is the value of dense environments: compaction imbalance is a key to civilization as well. The bond between any two humans is as vast and electrically charged, and just as deeply and mysteriously enfolded, in the archives of their minds as between two adjacent parts of a hormone...."*

Astari Manuscript, Book IV,
*Fundamentals of Psychometry.*

*"Remember: the midbrain, at infrared (like the centrioles of a cell), is in a faster time frame than the neocortex."*

Astari Manuscript *(Ibid.)*

\* \* \* \* \* \* \*

Essay 6:

## Apple Facts.

Everything exudes a signature, and that is our saving grace: we cannot ever get so lost and confused and ashamed that we cannot find our tone again. This tonal quality, this "soul" -- our mid-conscious review of ourselves -- is our eternal insurance: the duplicates of our experiences are well-imprinted

125

morontially. We can push against the possibilities of eternity, certainly; even fracture ourselves schizophrenic in a trillion fireflies going off helter-skelter in misdirections to explore infinity. But in our phosphorescence we have a built-in tendency to adhere to central premises that each of our pieces mutually embody; the way honey-making bees returning from their fields will swarm in a hive, and fireflies light up a patch of trees in an ever moving constellation; the way our cells divide, but adhere together in fluids and tissues and organs of their unique specialities. There is no glue that holds us together, you know. It is pure sensitivity and cooperation.

But if there is a built-in design to *unite and expand* our several parts, there is also the strategy to *divide and conquer.* I can understand why science is addicted to numbers: it is the game of nature. It is the basis of mind, the way we reflect upon our makings and our Maker; the way a thought acts within and upon itself in proliferation of its ideations, like cellular mitosis. It is the basis of reflectivity: the way "God" in Unity, self-reflecting, duplicates, triplicates, and complicates Everything. Nothing sits still: everything reflects to a center, to a question; and deflects outward, to an answer; again and again, over and over. We find that our definitions liberate at first, but after awhile they confine. We divide again, and conquer harsher; unite our variables again, into something softer.

Remember what the future says: the past merely takes up space; a good idea will haunt us forever.


I.


Everything *sings* its presence, because *presence* itself is a kind of singing. A thing announces itself by *being.* It is easier to see in things that grow, *because* they grow: we know something significant and inexplicable is happening, because

126

*growing* is something we also do; we know what it is to be *on our way,* so we have that kinship with "living things" -- we are cut from the same eager mold.   But even the mineral kingdom resonates.  We know this in our bones, our most difficult stones to grow, to  which we more distantly relate.  Sing to a stone, and it shakes:  it resonates to ultrasonic sound, even sitting still, untouched,  and  unawake,  in  that,  like  all  things,  it  is frequency-made:  it *is* sound.  To our piggish eyes, still heavy with  the  low-grade  drink  of  some  sloppy  concoction  of consciousness, a thing only occupies so much space, which we compute as a vast nothingness.  But even eyes originate out of "nothing" stuff, and vision itself *permeates* every solid thing it idea-shapes.  Our senses have yet to grow to their full fruition; when they do, I suspect they'll see something Whole even in a grain of sand.  But I speculate.  I am more or less as short-ranged as the next man.

We  do  not  realize  how  much  we  compress  ourselves, nor how much of the Infinite goes into that compression.  Even our  very  molecules  are  folded.    The  fabric  of  how  many constellations, not to mention our own star, are folded into the intake of every breath, absorbed in the layers of the skin.  We are  as  spacious  as  space  itself,  but  closet  our  spacious intentions into corners and crevices because we have it in us so to concentrate the Allness of all we are, so to squander our Inheritance, yes, but also to replicate the wealth of the realms, we who turn the cosmos inside out, who *are* the cosmos turned inside out.  I mean, what is an atom but a swarm of ideas so fast and furious, with nowhere to go, that they crave each other and the  all-surround  of  *anywhere*,  and  set  to  work  immediately building *anything* at the slightest provocation if Idea.   Not a particum of dust would exist without God, but what is God without  intricate  evidence?    What  is  Existence  without proof of Itself in a sea of blueprints?  The quantum world is a troubling of thumbprints, a smear of galaxies in a house of remembrances of movement and murder, a bedroom pleasure and horror, a carpet covered in bits of mirror, a sunbeam through a basement stair where motes of coagulate air run about on missions of errantry. We cannot fetch a jar of apricot jelly from the terrible cellar without meeting ghosts from the moon from the era of Lucifer niggling the face, and who knows what other far off dustings of place. More than we know in every room lingers there to greet us.

And what of the open fields? What of the cities and hills? It is a small thing in the scale of things, our little world. It is really a *remembrance* of things more than anything else. Newness only exists in possibility, and possibilities are endless: they fill too much world. They compile world on world, overflowing froth at the brim, and foam at the sea -- it is hard to tell if I am breathing the tavern air, or the tavern is breathing me! I have a head for beer; an atmosphere for cigarette smoke, and masculine jokes, camaraderie, and barely suppressed boy-fears. It doesn't matter where I go, Someone is always lurking about, much bigger than all else put together, bursting at the seams. My little environment is pregnant with themes, and who is it that got her so fat with child? Ah, could it have been really me? I am drunk with delight and smiles: I will be a Father soon, with all that Fathers me. But I have miles to go before that Dream.

In my own way I am talking about the mansion worlds, and picking your brain to help me remember from whence we came. I'm not sure I can remember all by myself. I have never explained what I mean, have I, about these worlds? But, of course, how can I, ever? For something so close at hand and all about, it lies beyond my scope to show you what I am almost seeing: a closet full of Grandma's things, going back to Gettysburg, and Roanoke, and farther back, to the mists of things. Those are not just trees encircling the house, they are dusty cardboard boxes with ideas still tumbling out of leafy Sumer and Mesopotamia. I have a panorama here somewhere from the very first city ever built; when you turn it upside down the heavens shake. And even the future figures in, like a Turkish tapestry weaving itself from the mouths of generations looking our way, dreaming, but yet to speak.

The world is not what we keep thinking it is. We are what the world keeps thinking, in her own hope chest, her own think tank.

## II.

Everything reflects to a center, and from that heart deflects to a purpose, be it a seed, a chromosome, a thought, an atom, a man, a universe. There is nothing that exists in the natural world that does not offer up abundant evidence of this very phenomenon of reflectivity. Existence *is* reflectivity. We use the word "God" in our attempts to get to the inner sanctum of this -- the "Big Bang" for those who like to start from a physical point of compression -- but that very effort, in either case, is self-*reflective*. Like a universe, or a frog, or a seed of momentum, we are *acting within and upon our start,* replicating images at the speed of interest, leading and following after a serpent or a train of thought. We have got ourselves by our own kittens, and are pawing after every moth. We are sitting ridiculous in a tangle of yarns, reflecting upon our dispositions. So this is Eden: a stretch of imagination; a flash of excitement, between yawns. Could anything be more explicit: we are gods, in effort of replicating the Dot who started all this!

So silly of us; and yet so charming and unfathomably mysterious. "God," of course, was never a man in the sky; nor an omnipresent ghost spread out in vast aroma in some big honeysuckle pie, or a fog. The one idea is too simple and compact; the other too nebulous and spread out. Our spirituality is vague because we have largely ignored it, the reality of underlying strata of mind -- the *essence* of things reflected to our eyes as mere image aids. For some reason we became obsessed with splitting and counting things, like a boy with a magnifying glass on the trail of ants. God is a unifying Intelligence, certainly, but arranged throughout the administration of things as a plethora of cooperative intelligences; more than just a gaggle of fairies and angels sent hither and thither by Zeus on missions of errantry, but intermediaries of our own identity, spanning the length of our minds, and more: the taproots of our spirits presiding in the *Presence* of things. But we do not know our own densities, let alone the multiple dimensions of this Mystery. Evolution is not haphazard, a blind groping left to its own mistakes and devising. The prevalence of varying frequencies reveals the hands of others reaching back. Those on the faster tracks *have been at the starting gate; have followed the trail of facts.* The future reaches back in a guiding remembrance, as the past bumbles forward in cute ignorance, and the present moment is the overlap of this graphic and divine industry: *intersecting time-waves is how to locate where we're at.* The Creation is wisely administered under quiet authority, did you honestly not know that?

Not everyone is as slow and set back as we are; not all quantum fields as dense. We exist in a sea of relationships, and can have had no idea of the extent of our relatives. Reality is a thing of interacting frequencies. These are the apple facts in the garden of reason, in that the evidence of this is everywhere. But we are going to need a whole new mindset to really understand ourselves in such a continuum of Identity.

Reality, in part and in whole, is self-reflecting. Period. That simple statement is basically comprehensive of all science and religion. It explains the Trinity, or the threefold co-existents at the basis of anything, from quarks to gyrotational gravity pull. It explains the sevenfold laws and presences permeating the three-fold All. The universe is not empty and stupid space. It is all hair and character bursting out of every face.

The phenomenon of reflectivity, in its intimate relation to sensitivity (and thus to sense and sensory development), these are the themes that interest me. There are other entities far more skilled in this than all my arrogance informs me of, so we are not left without help. We are ourselves reflective; that is, retentive, impressionable, transmittive. Our very reality-material is spectral and emittive; self-balancing and self-replicating. This is illustrated for us at every turn -- as seen in the cross-section of an apple, for example; or of a cell in mid-phase of replicating. But *mind, too, is obviously reflective,* we just haven't grasped yet the extent of *reality* in this. We don't outwardly see, typically, the image aids deflected away from us toward our areas of fixation at light speed. We do not communicate with our own messengers, sent willy-nilly out to gather information from everyone.

So it is no great mystery why *spiritual reflectivity*, at the farther end, should be so mysterious, so especially difficult for us to comprehend. The irony is that we have our very origin in these highly reflective entities: we *are* them.

But who are *they?* And how do we get ourselves to reveal to each other who we really are?

We seem to be the phenomenon of reflectivity itself, personified. How richly or poorly, I guess, remains to be seen.

III.

There is something satisfying about a threesome.

A dot is but a point, and worse: a point made without a purpose. It is point-*less*. Without reference to at least a gazillion more like pieces, what is its relevance? But in terms of infinity, now we have pigments and coloration and instruments; now we have a symphony and the possibility of orchestration; of making masterpieces out of ideation; now we have the possibility, not only of environment, but of *self-creation*.

But any two dots in relation (a *line*) by themselves is not only *potentially* something, but practically *problematic*: a line is invasive, a link from here to there, like a road, but to what purpose? A line is a shaft; a spear; a sentence. It is not an argument, it is argumentative. It is contention. It is polarity, and opposition; the scales of judgment, but never balanced for long in any one direction. It is a blank line that begs a remark; a signature; an *anything*. It is a white wall that cries out for graffiti. There is relation, yes, but shot through with arrows from relatives: relationships gone to pieces. It begs for mediation.

But there is something satisfying about a threesome. A line bent into an arc has a threefold relation: knowing the ends, we can find the center. And following the curve of any arc will describe a circle: thus, the wheel of time encompassing its own space, drawn by a Reason, and for a reason, at its own pace. Seen *three*-dimensionally, it makes a sphere. Now we are getting some *Where*, that only needs to be fleshed-in. On three legs a thing can stand on its own underpinnings without falling over; can support a burden; can compute a reason; can resort to faith. Even our mythological gods were incomplete on their own: products of imagination, they begged a wife and son. Even the latest One comes as a set: the *Father* follows his *Word* into *Expression,* giving us the Trinity. I am reminded of a face looking into a mirror, a similar face looking back at him, both filled with curiosity, wonder, and consternation: "Who am I?" each face reflects to the other One. "Why, I am *Them!*" says the revelator to the real and to his revelation.

The law of reflection in threefold explication is everywhere: in the way opposite poles set in motion a sphere of dynamics greater than the sum of all who get dragged into their concatenations.    Nothing exists outside of All:    all are implicated.  Even gravity has a threefold-stratum, a threefold-pull -- in the worlds of particles, of relations, of potentialities (matter, mind, and presence, respectively).  Any two colors will blend to make a third, and any two tones resounding together will generate a chord:  and the third part of any polar pair is always unique in its own creation.  Three distinctive natures permeate all Nature.  Concept, percept, and observation are one mirror:  a *Three-Way Mirror.*

IV.

Mathematically speaking, there are seven relationships, and *only* seven, possible in a threefold nature:

1. A
2. B
3. C
4. A+B
5. A+C
6. B+C
7. A+B+C

These constitute a second tier of Intelligences in the organization of Creation, and their handiwork likewise is everywhere:  in the frequency spectrum enfolded in solar and stellar light and radiation; in the realm of harmonics that govern the musical and quantum worlds.  Light and sound happen to be two areas of frequency-translation on which we most rely, so it is easy to find evidences of the sevenfold organization of things using the senses of ears and eyes.  Other senses utilized so exclusively would presumably yield similar discoveries in their own media of sensation.  But what interests me just now is the

133

way the octave is woven into the human image, giving us seven tiers of mind, and seven bodies enfolded in one.

The human body is made possible, biologically speaking, through the interplay of three primary elements (carbon [C], nitrogen [N], and oxygen [O]) held together primarily through hydrogen bonds. The sevenfold schematic of the *primary relationships possible* between these Big Three, as done with ABC above, reveals the fundamental relationships between amino acid groups (C+N+O) in the production of proteins, enzymes, and hormones, in all cellular categories (nerve cells, skin cells, blood cells, etc.); one favoring the special dynamics of N with O, another with C and N, and so on. Carbon essentially provides the scaffolding, oxygen the mobility, and nitrogen the lighting. The rest of the elements are the building materials, with simple hydrogen as the mortar. The Builder, of course, is in the writing: how these letters are put together to form sentences, sentences to form a thematic architecture, architecture to form an infinite landscape of realities.

We are so convinced of our solidity, it does not occur to us to look underneath the layers of these transparencies. We turn the pages only as far back as the skeleton, as if that is the sum of our anatomy. But that is only the bedrock bottom. Permeating every fiber, from skin to bone, are varying systems of electrolyzed fluid; the denser the fluid, the more active the electrolysis; and electron activity generates heat: so everything we think, having an electrical signature, through *thermal momentum* is transferred across a quantum bridge: from the slowness of molecular motion, to infrared, to electron density (visible light), to ultraviolet, and x-ray, and gamma, and so on. And if an army can march across a bridge in one direction, who's to say it cannot return with reinforcements, or trouble, or both in one?

We act as if our bodies are citadels built of stone, with here and there a window or a door for sneaking something in or out. We refer to atoms as "building blocks," as if they were solid. But they are just frequencies converging in a soup of primordial and futuristic blueprints conveying a cathedral idea of ourselves to our friends! Who are we in our thermal bodies, at the speed of infrared? Who are we at the speed of light, in our electron or light-bodies? Who are we in the blueprints of our bluebodies, at the ultraviolet end? We know what we are wrapped up in a package; what are we should we come unraveled end to end? Or are we already?

It is difficult to accept the greater possibilities of our-selves. Yet, because we *are* woven of variable frequencies -- implying a spectrum of "informations" of thermal, electrical, magnetic, and acoustical signatures at varying momentums and densities -- that alone tells us we are multidimensionally arranged, coexisting in interpenetrating "times," in interpenetrating "spaces." We talk futuristically of "folding time" and "folding space": *we are time folding in on its folded space.* And we are barely touching upon the *spectral* nature of atoms here, let alone the *spectrum of mind* and the *heavens of presence.* Which is to say that we do not just *occupy* a singular environment, by our sheer bulk alone displacing everyone and everything in our single-headed approach to whatever we're after; rather, we are *folded into the variables that constitute space and time.* "Space" and "time" are not governing principals: they are what we make of them.

In terms of presence, we *permeate* these layers of variables. In terms of mind and physics, we *settle.* Our actual *experience* is determined by how much or how little we actually *include* of our multiple streams of perception in this field of forever. For some, a *river* is not enough to drink. For others, a trickle is already too much wine.

## V.

Space (particulates) can be measured by time, but time (frequency) can only be measured by our subjective experience of it, as an overlapping fabric of "space-time" within and around our dots and waves and excuses and reasons. No matter how we look at it -- as interacting frequencies, as electromagnetic moments, as particulates dancing around each other without a chaperone at impossible velocities -- we are confronted with the phenomenon of overlapping time-waves, in *layers* of reality, and we are ourselves the "local" and "distant" participants. We are our own ancestors and our own progeny, looking forward with a backward glance; and the other way around, too, I suppose. Either way, we hurl our voices across the chasm, but we are the echoes coming back with a modifying idea. We should pay more attention to those intuitions. They've come a long, long way to intrigue and annoy us.

We are trying to make a difference both ways: in our getting in, and in our getting out. Said another way, we are ascending and descending the ladders of ourselves (using the scale of up and down). The local part, feeling incomplete and utterly alone, screams out maddeningly, "But... how can this be so?" The distant parts think, but cannot say aloud: 'How can it *not* be so? Someone has to make it work.' But then there is the nitty-gritty work of making decisions. A plant, like a civilization, must be *guided* to know where to grow, so it leaps out ahead of itself to try and know in advance, and greets whole selves coming back in the ebb and flow of sea and sap of all things solar and all things green, and all things so and not so; it dreams of itself as a masterpiece of flower or weed or uncut grass, and replicates itself from the inside out as if it had the know-how all worked out for itself on its own T.V. screen. But I really doubt that a plant understands its own photosynthesis, any more than we human weeds understand the brilliance of our own ignorance (... or the photo-synthesis in our *own* cells, for that matter). Something luminous descends, and calls up something thick and viscous into vesicles. By and by, a seed emerges, and grows the same idea of fields from whence *it* grows, with little variance from season to season, population to population. To what purpose, though, is all this proliferation?

Who knows. But does a weed need a reason for being? Does a rose? Does a human being? All a seed ever asks is for a season. Only the harvest knows the reason.

*"A man is prolific and divine*
*Only to that extent to which he can stretch himself*
*To think he is;*
*Is mortal and weak only to that same measure*
*Of his lack of trying."*

**Cantos from the Ghost of Lincoln.**

*"In this day and age, it is probably the education, training, and development of our young mentalists that occupies our brightest minds; [gap in record]; the exploration of alternate realities, the new enterprise. Gone are the days when technology and capital were all the rage, in the days of our isolation and insecurity, our obsession with money and political economy. But modern technocracy, like the old democracies, is hard-pressed to restrain our most aggressive minds, who seem to tolerate no secrets and know no boundaries. The opportunities for reality-engineering are seemingly limitless. Intriguing new frontiers and civilizations are disclosed almost daily. Image constructions are now more populous than their projectors -- it seems nearly everyone has a cohort of personal runners these days! But the proliferation of these so-called 'elites' is growing at an alarming rate. The necessity for a system of equity and solid training in ethics is more urgent than ever. Too many over-enthusiastic mentalists, technocrats and progressors alike are making swiss cheese of our very fabric of [gap in record]. There is a time and a place for lunging forward, yes; but not this recklessly. There is also a time and a place for restraint. There is no personal liberty that does not also come with its natural endowment of neighborly responsibility; for what the World Mind cannot integrate will long be our most severe haunting."*

Astari Manuscript, Book I,
*Fragments from the First Academy Archives.*


\* \* \* \* \* \* \*


Essay 7:

# Aristocracy of the Common.


I.


There is an innate threefoldness to all things in life, to all processes of life. It is the essence of all proof of that which we have been bastardly calling "GOD" -- and grossly misperceiving; groping in our learned darknesses to comprehend the evidence of something profoundly "divine" at work deep in the substructures of life: in the constituent parts of all matter, all phenomena of energy, all core dynamics of consciousness. It transcends what we are, yet IS what we are; it flows in, and flows out, like the tides of the sea, like breathing, yet *holds* the records of our comings and goings in perfect geometric and symphonic form, that we call "reality." But what is reality? It is the constant, forever reiteration of the Great Breath in-forming and out-forming every breather. It is the mist on the winter windowpane of our best efforts at perceiving the galactic night.

As there are three parts to an atom, three functions of electricity or magnetics, three divisions of the psyche, so also are there three parts to society -- the *cultural,* the *political,* and the *economic.* Historically speaking, these three distinct characteristics of society have mutated over time, growing out of the threefold nature of individuals themselves -- *body, mind,* and *spirit,* in traditional parlance.

In more poetic terms, I think of this as the in-out rhythm or pulse of breathing, but on a social scale. By "culture" I mean all that pertains to self-relation, to self-enrichment -- the exploration, discovery, and expression of reality in *self.* The cultural sphere of society thus has a spiritual, or *essential,* core and basis, from whence springs our best attempts at industry and enterprise, the whole realm of action and exchange of human energies, which is defined as "economy." Between these two, like the fulcrum of a seesaw, lies the "political" sphere, or all that pertains to the idea of equity or fairness; the realm of law and government, which seeks the right-relationship between individuals in their abuse of one another. Governments, of whatever denomination (civic, religious, corporate, academic), ideally provide the external restraints of decency and fairness upon those who have yet to learn the internal ones.

These three distinctive social functions are funda-mentally separate, *and should be kept so,* though obviously

142

coordinated as necessary, to fully serve the social ends for which they are (ideally) created. But that has not been the case throughout history. Indeed, we seem only now to be *beginning* to really distinguish between the separate functions of society -- only now really beginning to see society as a living *organism* in its own right. We have learned, rightly, to distinguish between Church (culture) and State, *and to keep them separated;* but we have yet to impose the same distinction and separation between State and Corporation, and between Corporation and Culture.

Value distortions relative to money have drawn a veil across our eyes, sending individuals, corporations, and govern-ments alike into staggering debts to one another; and we are beginning to repudiate the domination of economics and the intrusion of law into our private lives; but there is still great confu-sion as to which is which. The profit-motive which drives free enterprise keeps the pendulum swinging wildly between the financial interests of the corporate world and the public interests of conscientious lawmakers, so that the State and the economy tend to merge into corrupt reflections of each other. Often government seems to be no more than an extension of the corporate world, with politicians selling out to the bids of special interests, and corporations determining the laws of the land.

Culture, government, and economy are all vital to every society, but when one is allowed to dominate the others, the entire social organism suffers, as in a diseased state -- for one part of anything can only dominate *at the expense of the whole.* And the only way *any* institution can dominate the whole social organism is when *individuals themselves do not adequately look after their OWN interests.* In lieu of this, political and economic interests are always in contention over protecting and/or exploiting individuals who exercise little or no political and economic power of their own.

It should also be stated that State and Corporation are also comprised of individuals, obviously; but these are spear-headed by those who *do* variously empower themselves -- either to promote their own interests *at the expense of others,* or who lean more toward a public motive. Very often, I think, there is simply a confusion of the two motives.

A false-value system, introduced with the creation and manipulation of money (which actually has no intrinsic value at all), seems to be at the source of this confusion. Money has become the darling of every eye, and the poison in every brain. We live and die for that which, in the end, buys nothing of lasting gain, while we have lost something vital in the bargain, making us docile and sterile, complicit to our own servility, and in our ignorance chronically afraid.

With the circulation of money -- the substitution of *finance* for the system of natural economy -- a veil has been drawn over the whole economic life. The *perceived* value of the dollar takes precedence over the *actual* value of the individual. That is, the individual became *devalued* while money became the basis of economy. Everything now comes with a *price*, as if that was the natural order of things; a social inevitability. But it is a great error to confound the value of a service or commodity by its arbitrary price; and a great error to confound the value of a person by his or her wage or salary -- the "price" of the person.

Still, there is some light on the horizon. To paraphrase Rudolf Steiner, who has written extensively on the subject, "In the old days, the entire man was sold as a commodity. Today, only a remnant of the human being -- his labor power -- is stamped with the character of a commodity."

Thus, a confusion of boundaries exists between what is legitimately a part of the political sphere, and what belongs to the cultural and economic spheres: a person's *rights* and *values* are absorbed into the economic process of *buying and selling.*

So it begs the question: How can we differentiate and rightly coordinate these distinctive functions of the social organism under such a drunken stupor?

We have first to aright ourselves as individuals, reclaiming our own threefold functions of body, mind, and spirit; then society will automatically reformulate itself in resonance with the quality of being of those who comprise it. It is only a dog-eat-dog world because we have reduced ourselves to the status of dogs. We denigrate ourselves for our failures of body, mind, and spirit, and thereinafter must do battle with nearly everyone, blindly fighting for our relevance with those who think us more or less irrelevant -- irrelevant to *their* purposes is what this always means -- because we have lost sight of our own intrinsic value. We are conquered by a self-perception, not fully realizing that our only battle is with ourselves.

We are also a tampered species, and that has been especially difficult for us to admit to ourselves, as it is difficult to remember a childhood trauma when growing up under the alcoholic breath of a demonic father is the only "normal" we have ever known. We accept the truths of church and history at face value, for why should we not? The mechanical explanations of science, the simple arithmetic of economics, these are the pennies of intelligence one simply drops into the slot at the top of the head when that is the only allowance that has ever been given. We must first secure our bread; then, if there is time, and motivation, we will tend to more important things. So we tell ourselves. But we watch the seasons come and go, occasionally noticing the colorful little pieces of our dreams slipping away with every snowmelt. We are not certain just who our nemesis really is, but now that hardly matters. Parasitic worries that have no reality now but in our heads. Solar winds

145

have been unleashed into our sails; and those who once abducted us from our beds have become the hunted now.

History is not really the best sort of neighborhood to go exploring in to get a proper idea of ourselves; it has been tampered with; it never tells a truthful story, but reflects upon us like a circus mirror, showing only exaggerations and avoidances. Nonetheless, it throws out interesting images that can teach us *something*, if only how to laugh at ourselves. *Natural* economy I understand -- the necessity of food and tools, the exchange of information, the pooling of curiosity that drives human industry and innovation. But there is nothing natural about money. Who first introduced the idea was no real friend.

Finance has always masked the ulterior motives of calculating men. It has never had a truly public aim, but a bottom line of self-interest, perfectly mirrored by its monetary *rate of interest.* It is a barbaric practice that obscures the *real value* of exchange-worthy commodities and services for an arbitrary *number value* that usually has no relation to reality at all. The reality is that people have intrinsic value, have a right to life. The delusion represented by the false-value system of money is that people are worthless, that *things* have value, that *things* have a right to exist, but worthless people must *purchase* these things, even if they are necessary to life. In the false-value system, everything is *assigned* its arbitrary value according to mere numerical standards -- a cold, calculating logic that *devalues* human life, *uses* human labor and ingenuity for personal gain at the expense of another's freedom and happiness, and *deprives whole societies of the necessary things and conditions for a sustainable life.*

Money actually has nothing to do with economy, which is simply *exchange of energy between individuals.* Money is only a *medium* of exchange; but a medium so regulated and manipulated as to disallow other media of exchange, and distorted into the perception of being a commodity in its own right. But the distortion is only a distortion of *perception*. Societies trained into disempowering beliefs, into the devaluation of themselves, dutifully sacrifice their lives for these scraps of false value, and believe they have no choice. Again, they are only conquered by a self-perception: a perception of themselves as having little or nothing of any real value to offer to other human beings. So they sacrifice and slave for that which, in their confusion, *does* have value: money, and what money can buy. They have little or no concept of the *exchange-value of their own energy ... except as that is defined by the numerical value of a wage or salary -- the "price" of their qualities.*

That exchange can occur between individuals without resorting to another's scheme of interest-bearing credits and dollars -- *that one might actually possess qualities desired by others* -- that this is actually the natural basis of "economy," is a great simplicity that is lost in all the mathematical complexities of finance, of wage schemes of financial predation, and of self-devaluation.

One can simply chalk this up to human ingenuity, to the product of creative imaginations that simply ran afoul of human depravity -- greed and manipulation for superficial power; the struggle of unbalanced minds for the semblance of superiority, of *relevance*. But that does not explain the numinous hold that money has had on our minds, throughout our known histories, as if it were completely natural for primitive societies to obsess about gold. They do not. They only ever used it for mere adornment, because it was shiny. As a medium of exchange, we could just as easily, and more conveniently, have used clay tablets -- which, in fact, is just how it all began. It was obvious to all, back then, that "money" had no intrinsic value of its own, but was only a token of commodities in transit; only worth the commodities it represented. But when *metals* were introduced in place of clay medallions or papyrus or what have you; and when these metals were assigned *arbitrary numerical values of their own;* furthermore, numerical values *that could be altered and manipulated through schemes of surplus and scarcity,* as is standard operating procedure today -- a false economy was created that greatly obscured our sense of what economy naturally is: the exchange of energy. We think it has something to do with money. But that is a system of *prices*, not of innate values. The real value of a service or commodity has nothing whatsoever to do with any number value. It has only to do with the satisfaction of a desire. *Real value is relative to the needs and desires of human beings.*

The fundamental flaw that is so cancerous to economies -- expressed as the fluxuations of prices and interest rates of financial markets -- is the devaluation of human beings in their exchanges of energy one with another. It is not the devaluation we suffer in the perspective of those who but use us, or who dismiss us as being irrelevant to their designs. It is the way we devalue ourselves; the way we sell ourselves to market for a basic rate of exchange, as if we had nothing more to offer other human beings but some monotonous labor, and deserved nothing more than a bare subsistence. It does no good to blame the Church with its dogma of sin, its tyrannous Judge, its hatred of Earth and humanity, and its longing for the End. It does no good to blame science with its dogma of random occurrence, its accidental universe, its utter annihilation of individual relevance, its hatred of all that it cannot measure, cannot conquer. Deep down, we know we are to blame ourselves for our misfortunes and our failures. We want to do better. We want to arouse the dragon of power within ourselves, and dazzle with brilliance of idea and word and performance and style. We know there is something in us, a region that we have not tapped, that science and religion by and large know nothing about, and no interest in learning in their headlong conquest after a devoted following. But we are confused and afraid, and our obsession with the false security of someone else's money keeps us so.   With every purchase our basic insecurity becomes more obvious:   there are not enough distractions to buy that can long hide us from ourselves  Our flaunting of the standard "wealth" becomes an insidious social embarrassment: it only reveals the measure to which we have deluded ourselves in our bottomless appetite for social materials.


II.


Looking back over more "recent" history -- say, from the medieval organization of the "Three Estates" (the clergy, the nobility, and the commoners) to their modern industrialized versions -- it is as if these three faces of ancient society were each more or less blindly seeking their own autonomy and coordination.   Yet the current manifestation of these three estates in the cultural, political, and economic orders is still an *undifferentiated* and *uncoordinated* mess to some degree.  Their functions are *not* being clearly differentiated or defined, and relationships are still a contention of wills, with the result that the spiritual wellspring of the cultural sphere remains largely underground, unengaged, while the political and economic spheres overlap in a back-and-forth struggle of confusing voices and neglected or over-reaching responsibilities; each seeking domination at times, reconciliation at other times, like a bad marriage.

In feudal times, the lord was looked up to by the surrounding commoners, who looked to him for protection, and owed to him their service and fealty, *because men could not at that time make their individualities felt.*   The Church set the tone, the nobility set the clime.   The commoners carried the stones for the catapults.

Over time, as trading began in earnest and religion became more farcical, wealth and knowledge accrued, new inventions began to change industry, sophisticated financial mechanisms appeared on the stage (private ownership, investment capital and the quest for profit, the credit/debt fiasco, risk potentials, insurance), *and men could now make their*

149

*individualities felt in a more pervasive way.* So that now, in modern times, for all the abuses of power and privilege, and the relative impotence of the Church, the opportunities for the "commoner" to make his (and her!) own nobility and validity felt is more pervasively perceived to be *a matter of personal will and choice.*

With these changing conditions and attitudes of society on the whole, the threefold functions of the social organism have slowly evolved, ever seeking clearer differentiation and better co-ordination, yet is still something of a three-headed monster pulling in different directions at the same time.

Why is this?

Imagine the situation if the drones in a hive of bees began to hoard all the honey to themselves, overworking the worker bees to harvest more pollen and manufacture more honey, thereby straining the patience of the queen mother and her little aristocracy, who could not possibly pass enough legislation to maintain order against such voracious appetites and rampant greed. But that has basically been the situation in our modern societies: economic forces have always dominated the weakling culture, *because it is weakling,* and political forces have ever had to step in to defend these defenseless with a never-ending barrage of regulatory laws and agencies. Like an overprotective mother trying to come between the insecurity of her children and an abusive father, a servile population tends to get knocked about in the in-fighting between opposites -- between Big Government on the one hand, and Big Business on the other. (Since the Inquisition, one never hears mention of Big Religion.)

But the problems of capitalistic societies cannot all be pinned upon the profit-motive of economic entities (seen as *greed)*; nor upon the intrusiveness of overprotective regulators (seen as *social justice* and *national security*). Societies themselves bare the brunt of evils *because it is predominantly the ignorance, the insecurity, and the servility of individuals themselves that make them so vulnerable and plunderable to economic predation and political intrusion in the first place.*

150

Strong individuals do not just drift willy-nilly like ducks on a pond, going where they are told; they enter the fray and, for their own part at least, change the nature of the game.  It is the infantile elements of societies, the chump-change, that beg to be plundered, and then snivel for bully protection.  But what servility really needs is maturity, and maybe a little muscle of its own.

And time has a way of working these things out.

There is a kind of breathing rhythm in the long historical cycles:  the "inbreath" of all that is being taken in by the individuals of a given time frame; the "outbreath" of new industry and initiative.  The long, slow evolution from despots to democrats has been a labored breathing at almost every step, but we have trodden on.  The titans of industry have been in our midst a kind of tuberculosis of the lungs, whilst we carried their mansions on our backs like a good working class; yet they have also been our kick in the pants:  from stone guilds to industrial farms and factories, to street brawls and labor unions and revolutionaries; to modern entrepreneurs, the self-employed, the pacified and cubicled nine-to-fiver:  if our lives are generally mean and average, we have come some way.  It does not say a lot, perhaps, at the end of each working day, but looking back at all that way seems to imply that we have accomplished something.

It is as if we have had our minds set upon something, uneasily fidgeting with our hands, unable to articulate it; a troubling of crows in the branches squawking up a weak defense about something gone awry, a bully episode gone from laughter all the way to gasping accidental murder on the very playground of our pre-adolescent days, before we knew how to plan; and now our silence makes us co-conspirators, and centuries together have found and bound us into mute friends.

We do not talk much about it, but the Church has long been dead.  And something of ourselves went out with it.

Something in medieval man betrayed us all; clung to its antiquated ways of ritual and dogma, shuffled to hide the dagger, passed it along from friend to friend.  Nobody remembers anything, yet here we all are standing around without a song, a

151

hang-dog confession on every glum expression. Everybody frowns for the poor little savior-boy laying on the ground. Just a lump of hand-me-downs now, not even the evidence of any visible skin from where I stand. Which is to say that, whatever the reasons for the constrictive mindset of the Church of our ancestral ways, what free spirituality was felt in those days was pushed underground -- into repression and denial. Culture became Latinized, and disappeared; something vital went out like a snuffed candle, and even when the Dark Age came back on the world was still mortally startled. Ritual and politics prevailed in place of what had been too abruptly knocked in the head and killed: if a liberal and authentic spirit of free episode ever threatened to rear its freckled face, if a peasant ever showed an inexplicable grin, it was straightaway clubbed again, first with brutal persecution, then with smug ridicule; today, with the needle of indifference.

This very generation we are the numerous inheritors of this ancient guilt: we snicker at anyone who dares to presume to an honest spiritual experience, for then we stand before a living mirror of our own impenitence.

But something else occurred along the way, which no burgher or nobleman or village priest of the day could have foreseen: that fountainhead of personal and free spirit that got repressed, re-emerged in a distorted, unconscious current of *scientific intellectualism* and *financialized economy* -- an aggressive, enterprising spirit that looked to flesh alone; an obsession with counting dots and amassing dollars -- notions of risk and risk management, of securing credit (debt), of insuring against the upsets of nature and enterprising capital: a new spirit arose to drive industry relentless, purely intellectual, just as the original intuitive was stealing away, secretive and forgetful. Spiritual values became dollars and cents; meaningfulness became more and more but meaningless routine. Then aroused the labored breathing of industrialization, the back and forth pendulum swinging of restrictive law and government, taking over for the dying Church, to try and contain, yet aid and assist, the blind, enterprising force of economy on the scent of money, progress, and prestige; the wheezing of need and greed, rich and poor equally obsessed with mere

152

accounting; for money, which is but a symbol -- a *medium* of external exchange -- became the thing itself, the mirage of oasis in a barren sand of time. Men looked to the material world only, to what lay all about them; for what was of *real* value, that lay internal to the mind (in the creation of its own *experience*), was claimed as the exclusive property of the Church; but the Church neglected its stewardship of the sacred, for the mere sacramental; but curiosity toward money and matter were not heresy: the door to higher culture closed, but the way was wide open for everything else.

Today the individual, rich or poor, intellectual or experiential, who labors to aright himself from the awkward position of having to *deny* his very core and source, forgotten after long centuries of ignoring it, now lives in a hollow and trying manner to fill up the inexplicable void of monotonous and redundant living, still not realizing that nature is but the projection of nature's Source; that a mind must create its own version of reality for there to be an environment to go exploring in at all. All are caught up in a dream of images, and even the images are dreaming galore, splitting off of one another in fractals alike from geniuses and idiots.

In all these long centuries, *scientific intellectualism* has ever been the real "achievement," for that is what has given us industrial machinery and capital. It has given us modern convenience and technology. It has, to some degree, liberated us from the hazards of living in a predatory world, except where it still ensnares us in our own tedium.

*But there was electricity before there were wires, and ambition before there was industry.* In the final analysis, our mighty intellectualism but *mimics* with technical objects what life itself already employs, *without* wires and circuit boards and computer chips, ropes and pulleys, levers and motors, and human imagination and industry. Someone was here before us, for the whole universe already runs like a well-oiled machine, without a single mechanical part. Ingenious! We secondary divinities have developed a great and useful facility for origination, *but we always had the electrical nature, the frequencies, the flexibility to know all microscopic and telescopic things.* We can

153

employ the tools of reason to design, create and unleash the bare beginnings of an internet, because *we Are the world wide web*: we are self-reflective entities who have come to know ourselves in the only way that was free for us to explore: through the exteriorization of our deeper industries.

But whatever became of the pure part that was driven underground, that became afraid to surface?

*There are two sides to history.*


III.

Society becomes two dimensional -- a mere tug-of-war between business and politics -- when its third dimension, the cultural sphere, is pressed so thin as to become invisible.

Education, for example, a facet of the cultural sphere, dominated by both economic and political intentions, is largely regarded as training for the workplace -- the economic sphere; yet public education is greatly hampered by governmental regulation as a preventative measure *against* economic vulnerability. But from a purely cultural perspective, *education is to enlighten and empower individuals in and for themselves*, irrespective of how they may later shape up to be good workers and logicians serving the purposes of other men. Ultimately a society is better served when its people can hold their own against economic leaders who really just want to use them, and political leaders who feel it their responsibility to protect them as if they had no other kin.

The culture has its leaders too, of course, but they are generally as ninny as all the others under their daycare; so that in the churches, for example, (a major facet of the cultural sphere) a similar dynamic is played out as in the larger society: a fairly docile congregation pays its tithes and abides, abides, abides by the glorious legislation handed down from on high, and never bucks the system with an unauthorized question: religious economy and polity dominate these mental factories much the way civil economy and polity dominate the larger community and society as a whole. It is just business and regulation on another scale.

Or look at the way scientists are constrained to prostitute themselves to political, military and economic interests for the sake of funding and prestige. Scientific exploration is as vital to a healthy *culture* as is education, religion, or the arts; but because the cultural sphere itself is so pervasively dominated by those with political and economic agendas, scientific minds are steered by political and business minds into the development of weapons and drugs and entertainments, profitable hospitals and other business enterprises, and the profit-motive hijacks vital public interests meant to benefit the *whole* society, not just the desperations of a few.

Independent artists, writers, and inventors generally fare the worst financially, perhaps, among the cultural lot, unless they're "discovered" in a big way, or have the wherewithal to ride out the hard years of their solitary apprenticeships. This very independence, however, makes them unexploitable to business enterprises, and irrelevant to civic leaders and hard-pressed people. Otherwise, they will swell the ranks of advertising agencies, newspapers, machine shops, the building trades, where their talents are marginally useful or never mentioned. Many a poet, dancer, novelist, sculptor, painter, actor, weaver, linguist, inventor, and dreamer languishes in a cubicle for a paycheck that keeps one solvent, serviceable to the profit-margin of a corporate or industrial leader, but self-betrayed and hollow in the center, living by rote but without real purpose and meaning. Such is the price of a niggling fear.

All in all, the cultural sphere is a severely deflated balloon compared to the robust spheres of political and economic enterprise, however demeaning it may be to the little guy. This is a generalization, of course; there are failing businessmen and weak politicians as well, and there are admirable cultural leaders somewhere, I presume. But on the whole, the cultural sphere is alternately dominated by the economic and political spheres, pointing up the need for greater public awareness of the *existence* of a threefold nature to society, of the symbiotic relationships between them, and the urgency of our best minds to cooperate in creating distinctive cultural organs that can vie with political and economic forces; and thereby coordinate with civic and business leaders *as an equal partner,* among those in each sphere who truly do care about other people (the greater wellbeing of the whole society), to right the imbalances of our current societies.

The churches are far too parochial and archaic to serve as effective cultural organs but to a small percentage of the population.  They are still useful and desirable centers for some.  Many people, however, myself included, find their programs spiritually offensive and ecumenically self-serving.  The universities cannot really serve in the capacity of real cultural organs either, for they are basically extensions of the other spheres, serving counting, stacking, and hacking purposes.  Science has no cultural organ outside of the universities and observatories, having been "abducted" wholesale for military and industrial purposes of the lowest order.  And museums and art galleries are for tourists.  Even sports arenas are mere extensions of the economic sphere, big money-making affairs.  So where are to be found the cultural organs to combat the dominance of government and business, to bring a better balance into human affairs?

As I look out from my roost upon these sordid affairs of so many servile human beings, who give up so much for the sake of a skeletal share of the continental bounty, it sometimes angers and sickens me, for I am also prone to blaming it all on self-serving politicians and rich businessmen.  I usually identify with the little guy, for like many of them I have never been eager to take advantage of the down-and-out, or the weak, or the ignorant, for the sake of some personal advantage.  And it's difficult for the little guy to admit to those embarrassing but obvious things about ourselves:  that for all our encyclopedic knowledge and argumentative logic, our modern societies are suffering from a deplorable lack of interest in simple and vital ethics; a rapidly declining intelligence, especially in spiritual matters, hardly keeping pace with scientific intellectualism; a kind of antisocial arrogance; retarding religious beliefs in sin and sacrifice that are repressive to self-esteem and self-confidence, despite the "chosen people" status of these social clubs; and a general apathy and fear of responsibility in the face of exploitative jobs and invasive regulations. We do not even stand up to the obvious criminality of pharmaceutical companies that are circulating deadly drugs into the populace without restraint, because we are a drug culture: we believe in the power of the pill, but not of the will. A large proportion of the populace is still relatively infantile and dependent. Period. How else to explain a civilization of peoples so nationally insecure and economically servile?

We do what we do for the daily dollar because we are yet too ignorant and too insecure to do otherwise. We have yet to create the vehicles to *enable* us to do otherwise.

And why are we so scatter-brained and frightened to do this thing? Because evolution is a slow affair. Only yesterday we allowed an arrogant and abusive Church to dictate how we would think and choose to live our lives. So we have come some way in our explication of ourselves. We have largely mastered our tyrants and our monarchs through the gradual arousal of the idea of *natural rights* in a few good heads, setting to rout the notion of the divine right of only the privileged few. We have evolved a kind of lazy man's republic -- a limited democracy. We send representatives of ourselves to legislate and exercise restraints so we don't have to. We have become, to that extent, more enterprising. It used to take a club for an intelligent man to get the mob galvanized enough to build a pyramid; now we'll volunteer to build a bank, at least, for a semi-respectable wage. More and more heads are starting to get it, that we are innately tapped into something electrical and magnificent; and more are brimming over with good ideas, and with the wherewithal to share and implement them. The grunt still feeds his appetites, dips his wick wherever he can, does his share of the daily sacrifice for a share of the drippings, and matures a little with age. All will die in a miserable heap on a damned hospital bed and come back more resolute about this business of becoming genuinely respectable. We all look forward to becoming, you know, maybe, a little wise.

In the interim, we are getting there a bit more slowly.

## IV.

I believe that in some unquantifiable, transcendent way, long historical cycles play themselves out in the shorter historical fractals of each person's individual life, and *that* played out between the life and death of each day; the way tiny wavelets can be seen to ride on the slower waves lapping in from the deeper depths, and even microscopic waves atop the wavelets. A pond or a lake, and the whole world's ocean too, I guess, is an open book that tells a vaster story than any one of us can take in at a single glance; every motion in the All-surround, and down in the depths, and even in the quiet heights, is there recorded. And so it is in the mind of a man or woman reflecting upon a singular occurrence, the whole momentum of which carries all the subtleties of centuries of imagination and achievement, of time-waves overlapping in every moment, and civilizations enfolded in every minutia of seismic attitude.

The narrow range of our imaginations today (for we are mostly repetitive, living on automatic), constricts the vital forces of the greater spiritual life into antiquated ideas and beliefs and rituals of hyperactive intellectualism obsessed with its facts -- with numbers and ballots and dollars and bullets, commodities, commodities, commodities, score cards and lotteries, and all manner and points of argument. Thus we hurl ourselves through a day, from its morning Inquisition to its daylong industry and haze, unto its evening buffet of news and entertainments; until old age snoozes in its easy chair, suppressing a long frustration and impatience that has long become etched in the face, because in those moments when we sensed our potentials we dismissed them to a future date. All our lives, it turns out, we were mostly dreaming of better days; and all the while, on the other side of the veil of every dream, *actualities* that we could not see but in our mind's eye were staring us in the face.

All for want of scope of a *trained imagination.*

But here's the kicker. Though we perceive in a one-line development sort of way, any experiment in altered perception indicates that the broader reality is actually more richly arrayed.

Environment is a *layered* thing that can be perceived in multiple ways. The long historical cycles, in all their variations, and their extensions into long futures seemingly out ahead of us, these are reflected back to us, very subtly, in the fractal of every day. *If we were more elastic and selective tuners,* we would be able to discern a wide variety of subtle impulses showing us how the future grand achievements and abysmal failures are shaping up for us even in this very hour, in this very space. It is not so much a question of evolutionary stages, as of *subtle attunements.* We must train ourselves back into imagination -- our cosmic and cultural roots.

We think the entire momentum of consciousness flows in one direction only, into an undeveloped future -- toward a dream of civilizations yet to be created. *But only by the splitting of perspective can this be made so, for experience is a thing of* **consciousness** *more than a thing of atoms and stones.* Yet there is always another momentum that flows opposite -- *many,* in fact, from *all directions* -- that interpenetrate each other at different frequencies, like radio waves. Because we *perceive* ourselves so singularly, we digitize this spectral mix into particles -- little packets of other bits, all arrayed according to differentials of frequencies: differing *time-flows.* In broader terms, atoms are not stationary at all, and we are not isolated singularities, or clumps of flesh and bone. We are the eternal holograms of ourselves, venturing "out" into the realms of every conceivable possibility; extending ourselves; multidimensional in our "layering" of potentials; selective focusers in a field of multiplicities. We hurl ourselves environmentally into the ALL, and go out to meet ourselves coming and going in the wild mysterium racing about in every particle of our perceiving, and peeping out of every face.

We are not at the top of some pyramid at all, nor on the frontal wave of evolutionary momentum, for elsewhere we are already "evolved" and working backwards to guide the moments of our ethereal grace. Our blind assumption has been that in our human stance we have achieved the greatest summit of intelligence so far achieved by any race; but this has been our greatest blunder: for a mind that presumes to be on top never considers who might be overlooking it with better advice.

Spirituality is not just an intellectual aspect of our culture, like reason or morality. It is the very wellspring of the natural world, making all parameters of reason and morality possible. It is therefore the basis of relationships in all spheres of society -- in political and business relations, as well as in cultural clubs like churches and schools and laboratories and artistic circles. It is the relegation of spiritual realities --*one's own soul life!* -- to the status of a mere abstraction, having only an ethereal quality, if any reality at all, that robs the individual of his imagination, inspiration, and intuition; weakens him into a chronic poverty and servility before more aggressive men. Culture is a reflection of the *spiritual vitality* of the people, or of the lack of it. The current political and economic morass would change if the people involved in this bipolar relationship, rich and poor, were to be infused with a new spiritual regeneration welling up from within. Only then can the cultural sphere take its place as an equal, *recognized* power beside the other two functionals of the social organism.

When one stands in the *presence* of the "superreal," as opposed to the merely obvious, or to the subreal; when the high-frequency domain, not of energy now, but of *intelligence*, is no longer held at a distance by the intellect, then one gains a new vantage ground on reality, for it becomes obvious just how *saturated* one is within it.

It is as if we find ourselves sandwiched between an ethereal reality above (considered essentially *unreal*), and a visceral reality below (usually considered to be *too real* -- too dumb, or too terrifying in possibilities to be blundered into) -- whereas we occupy a mid-realm, believing ourselves to be at the summit. But we are really just being intellectual, not real at all except in the most mundane ways. We are basically oblivious to the fact that there are happenings in *upper strata* of our minds -- for higher frequencies are *ethereal* to us, not visceral, not obvious -- where we are actually *between* upper and lower strata. Thus, not acknowledging even the *existence* of upper strata except in the most ethereal of ways, *we presume to occupy the upper strata ourselves, and this is the basis of religious and scientific pretensions to exclusive knowledge.*

Our arrogance has been a protective sheath that masked a great historical damage done to ourselves.

To know what the future is telling us, we must widen our imagination and see what falls into view on the momentum of inspiration and intuition. This does not negate the functional value of the intellect, but rather complements its linear logic with a depth-perception which abstract thinking alone cannot give us. Abstract thinking stands apart from direct experience. In old Europe, because free spiritual inquiry and exploration was not countenanced by the Church, education into law and medicine and theology and economics became increasingly mechanical and lifeless. Spirituality that has only the power of abstraction dries up the living culture of society, leaves only the dry husk of an older culture behind, depriving the current generation of its *own* innate vitality, for the wellspring of its very consciousness is being dismissed. Thus, the energy of the succeeding generations, neglected, denied, ignored, forgotten, became an unconscious drive in the realms of politics and economics, in an even stronger intellectualism, industry, and financial hunger: a blind *lust for progress* that concealed the real, but denied, *lust for life*.

The problems of our global societies -- *a deep insecurity in the populace, greed in the marketplace that will do anything for a buck, and presumption in government* -- these are deeply endemic, but still remedial: through the creation and proliferation of cultural organs rightly differentiating between the three distinctive functions of the social organism, yet also coordinating their separate functions so as to enhance the quality of life for all concerned. To do this, **the profit-motive must be made sub-ordinate to the service-motive**; but this requires a truly encultured people -- spiritually adept, so to speak -- with access to a political might and economic leverage of their own, independent of, but complementary to, established political and economic systems.

Without a real immersion into the true expanses of the *Self* -- not in an abstract-philosophical or sentimental-religious way, a mind still holding itself back from actual experience, but

161

in a direct, experiential way -- culture has no enlivening spirit; individuals remain wan and two-dimensional, at the level of their abstractions, but not vitalized; more in the character of limp noodles than live wires; who perforce remain sterile and anesthe-tized by the addictions of their virtual reality games. Such people cannot vie with the strength of those who *do* engage the Self in more than an intellectual way. Altered states of consciousness (naturally induced), explorations across the threshold of nightly dreams, and so-called out-of-body excursions -- these are the primary ways in which the Self can be explored and discovered, its vast reserves tapped for personal or altruistic pleasure, beyond the mask of contemporary personalities. *These are the ways in which an individual and culture in general are best revitalized.*

Without Spirit, by whatever terms and whatever means, there can be no practical sovereignty but in the mechanizations of the State; and without practical sovereignty, there can be no genuine stewardship or ministration of the real needs of a community, only sentimental overtures made by a flock of sheep, while the predators continue to use the precious time and strength of their fellowmen to serve merely private purposes, as if they alone were entitled to liberty and security, food, and a space of time in which to calmly think.

Enterprise is not the privilege of the wealthy, but the innate capacity of *all* people -- for people are naturally endowed with the vital force that animates industry, and given time and suitable conditions, they will come to know this about themselves.

I my conception of a *stewardship guild*, I envision the beginnings of a higher type of humanity, and the kinds of organizations that might help get us there; and I understand that to offer such a model is an exercise in futility where the soil is not prepared to take the seed; that dispirited beings will go on being whatever their lowly conception is. Yet I also believe in the strength of ideas. There is a need for a new cultural endeavor to raise contemporary men and women up out of their needs, out of their apathies and entrainments. Spirit alone gives dignity and power to an honest mind intent upon a meaningful life.

## V.

## THE STEWARDSHIP GUILD

It is not difficult to conceive how a stewardship guild can function:  it only requires enough security in its participants to release them from the financial treadmill of daily survival; *to release their innate desire to contribute from their strengths, rather than feeding their frenzies.*  In the total environ of such contributions, private needs are variously met, thus diminishing (if not outright erasing) the necessity of using money by removing the cost of staple necessities -- housing, food and water, energy, and the raw materials and labor required for industry and new invention.

Once *security in the populace* is redressed, the other two major weaknesses in the economic and political spheres can be effectively combated:  *greed in the marketplace,* and *presumption in government.*  Then it is a matter of coordinating the distinctive functions of the three social spheres -- cultural, political, and economic -- so that no one of them is allowed to dominate the others.  Economic predation is effectively checked, not by over-protective and intrusive government, but *by a self-motivated workforce of individuals looking after* **one anothers' interests** -- body, mind, *and* spirit.

A society can only stand up for itself by standing up for each other.

Until individuals learn to provide for the needs of others, society cannot rightly provide for the needs of individuals -- for society does not exist as something apart from those who comprise it.  In a world where everyone is primarily oriented towards securing the needs and interests of self, *and self alone,* the strongest will always ride roughshod over the weak.  But the "weak" individual is only one who hides from itself, who has not the sense of its innate resourcefulness, of its innate sovereignty.  A stewardship guild, as a model of the threefold social organism, only mimics the three-part nature of the individual -- for any given man or woman must be considered in terms of *body, mind,* **and** *spirit* to be realistically considered at all.  Anything less is but a *partial* consideration. And this is the mistake of our ancestral thinking, which often does not consider the whole person; many people do not even consider themselves in whole terms. People are not just workers and consumers and taxpayers and citizens, sinners and patients and students, voters and constituents. Each of these are bodily, mentally, and spiritually endowed entities, *innately resourceful and sovereign,* whether they yet understand this about themselves or not. And virtually *all* governmental regulation and economic exchange come down to the giving or withholding of *consent* between individuals. There is no such thing as "Big Government" or "Big Business" but in relation to *little humanity* -- a population in abject consent to anything.

For an individual to function well, the needs of the body must be coordinated with the needs of the mind and spirit. This is the same as saying, collectively, that for a society to function well the interests of economy must be coordinated with the interests of government and culture. Yet this is not really being reflected in either episode. Man and mankind alike are dominated by economic considerations almost exclusively.

Imagine if it were the other way around. It would be unthinkable for an individual to utterly ignore the needs of the body, and cater only to its intellectual and aesthetic interests, of mind and spirit. If a man shall not live by bread alone, he shall not live by head alone either, or by heart alone. But bread is more tangible than words and images, so overall economy tends to dominate the minds and hearts of men in the blindness of thinking that money makes the world go round. The world goes round by the governing laws of enterprising mind and spirit, not by economic forces. Money is just a social agreement made tangible between people who don't know any better. It is the debt of the banker passed off to the debtor. The bulk of it is not even paper! It is just the promises between two consenting makers -- creditor and debtor -- conjuring it out of thin air! Each is seeking to satisfy an appetite. But stomach alone does not suffer. There is a hunger of the mind, and a hunger of the soul, that economy does not but one-third answer.

It is not difficult to understand why each of the "three estates" (economy, government, and culture) must coordinate in turn with the overriding interests of the other two for there to be a properly self-balancing people. Only then can ALL be granted the economic guarantees now denied them, and a self-responsible citizenship roll back the encroachments of over-parenting governments, and societies be introduced to their spiritual foundations.

Where existing conglomerates and governments cannot easily make that shift to a threefold balancing or coordination of the three spheres of interest of society on the whole, small groups of individuals in public stewardship *can* provide such oversight for their local communities. This requires, in each guild, the creation of three distinct peer groups dedicated to their respective "estate," and three councils to coordinate the public endeavors of each peerage. All are *stewards* -- that is, motivated by a will to serve the needs of the whole, from a mindset of individual resourcefulness and sovereignty -- but working cooperatively *as they naturally fall in together as peers* in selecting the areas of greatest interest to them individually: in political, economic, or cultural endeavors. A judicial council then forms the seventh part of a stewardship guild, to mediate disputes and adjudicate any breaches of trust.

For simplicity's sake, I refer to the peer groups by nick-names -- "spooks," "scribs," and "grubs" -- and to the coordination councils by more elaborate names, as follows:

1. **Rights & Values Council** -- coordinating cultural and political projects (between spooks and scribs, respectively).

2. **Motive & Means Council** -- coordinating cultural and economic projects (between spooks and grubs, respectively).

3. **Commonwealth Council** -- coordinating economic and political projects (between grubs and scribs, respectively.)

To give a more concise picture of how a stewardship guild might function, consider these descriptions:

## PEER GROUPS

*Culture* is the realm of education, the arts, religion, and science (ideally) were they not under the domination of political and economic interests. It is essentially concerned with the **values** of society -- with intellectual, moral, and spiritual values. Those stewards who are drawn to the cultural peerage of a guild are primarily interested in cultivating the highest aspects of human nature -- the aesthetic and the spiritual, even to the divine core of the individual. These I call "**spooks**" in my homely analogies.

*Politics* is the realm of law and government, of public awareness and political action committees. It is fundamentally concerned with the issue of **rights** -- of the "unalienable rights" inherent in human nature, and those privileges granted by administrative authorities. Those stewards who are drawn to the political or legal peerage of a guild are primarily interested in social justice and public awareness, with influencing the laws of the land. They are the clarifiers of definitions and meanings. These I call "**scribblers**" or "**scribs**."

*Economics* is the realm of industry and invention, of business and finance, construction and farming. But by and large it is the realm of households, a fact all too easily overlooked in the profit-driven world of stocks and dividends. Economics is basically concerned with the practical affairs of daily living and social progress -- the realm of physical **needs**. Those stewards who are drawn most to the economic peerage of a guild are primarily interested in the practical concerns of securing the basic necessities of life that provide a solid foundation for the exercise of rights and privileges, and the pursuit of higher values -- indeed, the pursuit of excellence in character and in society. Most apologetically, I call these fine fellows of the dirty fingernails simply "**grubs**."

166

The inter-association of spooks, scribs, and grubs -- of *stewards* secure enough in themselves to answer the call to service and duty, not as others decide, but as they determine for themselves -- is the new aristocracy of the common. Presidents are not really as powerful and glorious as we like to pretend; they are just the glorification of all that we like to see ourselves slathered in, with a veto power instead of a paltry vote -- why so few of them actually inspire. They are the common denominator; no better and no worse, generally, than their brief tenure at the front of the line of their followers. When their tenure is up, we forget their names. Legislatures and judiciaries fare no better. These are all but representatives whose hour is almost over -- reflections in a mirror; secondaries. The hour of their sovereignty is brief, to the extent that their power is only delegated. Theirs is merely the scaffolding, not the State. *We* are the State. *Ours* is the sovereignty, for there is no other between Man and Mankind but what is meant to serve for a time in our ascent to Unity. What presidents and politicians mirror back to us by our consent, our delegation, and our complacency, we first commission by our timid but no less authentic and sole authority. We are the unstated presidents and legislators of the commons, the judicials of our privacy.

And what is all this confabulated money of the profiteer in the estimation of a revolutionary? In one dreadful hour it can all disappear; a worker's strike or a run on the bank, an electorate demanding a recount of votes -- when once the match is struck, the whole house of cards will go up in smoke. It has happened before; it will happen again. Republics are only as brave as they are broke. But when once they come awake and neglect their toils -- spook, scribbler, or grubber for dollars -- no swank cosmopolitanite in that long hour will get in a moment's honest sleep, for the whole world will be knocking at their golden doors.

The *needs, rights,* and *values* of society are best repre-sented by individuals themselves, when once they are free from the yoke of their insecurities. It is the self-appointed task of stewards to hold this ideal for their surrounding communities till more should awake; for how much longer, really, can the

167

inevitable be avoided? The contrast between the needs of commerce and the needs of ordinary people is completely arbitrary, unnecessary, a great imbalance that needs to be righted. The same may be said of the contrast between the so-called sovereignty of the State and the sovereignty of the voter. If only an understanding of selfhood and creator-power could be more easily received by the typical man in the street. Ah, well; that is the way it goes. The fat little caterpillar feeds on a leaf and goes to sleep. The butterfly needs only the nectar of a flower, floats on a breeze, and probably doesn't even remember chewing on green, or sleeping on the couch, or waking up with two very big impossible wings.

## VI.

Though I offer this little model -- a sketch, really -- of stewardship guilds and colonies in the hope that socially conscious people will by and by stumble upon them and be amazed, and utilize them in fleshing out their own intentions and dreams, in broader terms it is my deepest understanding that the world is already full to the brim and to the brink of overflow with the quiet working of public stewards -- of spooks, scribblers, and grubs already taking wing. I am a late comer in those terms. Already a vast army are on the march, honest seekers of something simple in a culture of deceits; looking to enlighten their own benightedness, if not their brother's; self-correcting their old insecurities; aiming straight enough to amend their crooked feet; to empower themselves by making a pretty difference in a world more defined by its ugliness -- a world which they helped to create. It little matters whether or not my terminology is used; there are other words that are just as good. But the basic model, you have to admit, is pretty damned neat.

In my finest hours I know that other people are essentially no different than me; that we all tend to vacillate between different faces, as if we were trying on shades. For myself, I have taken slow turns to be spook, scrib, and grub, all three: I spook out my ulterior motives and true values; I scribble out my words; and I grub for the dollars to survive while I put my message out to the world. In the end, I can do no more for others than I do for myself; and can do no more for myself than I *believe* I can.    But this is so far the finest fruit of my accumulated knowledge:   that as far and wide as I can see, there are nothing *but* stewards, and not one community or nation but what is virgin territory to these eyes, with a whole lot of good ideas slowly coming home to *me.*

*"A man either believes in himself, or he does not.*
*That is just about the barest fact of any matter.*
...
*A man encounters just about what he expects to get;*
*No more; no less.*
*He is his own engineer; or, backing down from the size of this,*
*His own inconsequence."*

**Cantos from the Ghost of Lincoln.**

AFTERWARD.

## Codicils and Colonies:
### parting thoughts toward a new world view.

The era of the nationstate, Allah be praised, is near to collapse, done in by its own torpor. It is already leaning over farther than the Tower of Pisa, propped up only by its habitual patriotism. The arrogance of nationalism stinks like a carcass, and the buzzards are circling overhead, indicating the death of something slow and inefficient. I doubt any nation will last a century. Something new is on the rise.

Skinny old patriots may still present themselves as our eternal guardians, but their memories are marred and scarred by wars and hatreds and outmoded beliefs. Nations are already antiquated systems anyway when concepts of world currency, the "global village," and world councils like the United Nations have entered the vernacular and commonplace. Only the present entanglement of political parties with financial markets, and the demoralization of their peoples (some still dominated by religious intolerance), keeps the old boundaries from being erased. They have *long* been unnecessary, really, and were always arbitrary to begin with, not natural features of the

173

landscape. Looking at ourselves from deep space, notice how the world is not demarcated into purple squares set beside green ones and red ones and blue ones and brown ones, with little hedges growing up in dotted lines, or rivers of oil emerging from crevices, to separate the peoples of the earth into black and white, or inferiors and superiors, and similar corrals. There is a little bit of every nation everywhere, almost in every face, pointing up the real indifference with which we patronize our own indigence. All our flag waving set aside, on our better days we know very well that no one nation is really any better than another; that all are but scaffoldings toward global unity; that there are no "chosen peoples" under modern grace.

But societies are built upon lies. Maybe that is over-stating it, but bear with me. Humanity has long lived under the assumption of vulnerability -- the predatory universe theory, basically. Our governments and churches have always reflected this back to us. They stand between us and our pretend "enemies". Our very *motive* for clustering into social circles has always been seen as self-preserving. It's what makes us so self-serving. Said another way, our institutions are geared to maintain the status quo, not so much in pursuit of their goals, but *to suppress the abilities of those who would throw off such limitations as the laws and beliefs of the mob impose.* Group-thought always undermines the integrity of the individual; for too much strength of individuality -- too much boldness, originality, and courage -- is a threat to vulnerability. There are those who require a holding pen, and those who bristle at the mere mention of handling.

I have trumpeted on and on about the superior advantages of personal sovereignty. I have directed your attention, over and over, to the spiritual core of your fundamental integrity. I have given you a splendid model of stewardship guilds and colonies, painting it so broadly that you would have to fill in the details yourself -- for the details of my vision are not in by-laws and Olympian structures to stand for all time, but in the nitty-gritty of individuality nesting between individuals. Society is not something to be built, it is what we *Are*. And economy is only the exchange of gifts between us. The question is: are we to carry on in our old conviction of vulnerability, charging interest, or are we to conjure a new world view predicated on something profoundly more honest and fearless?

Societies are built upon lies, in the sense that our vulnerability is an illusion. The notion of a predatory world is too nearsighted, seen only through the spectacles of frail little scribes, who have unfortunately been writing our constitutions and bibles. And this being also our education these many, many lives, we have naturally consented to be so governed, the better to protect our vulnerable little hides. We have burnt men and women at the stake, and sent whole families to the grave, who dared to suggest anything different.

Societies are thus not easy to change. *Perspective,* however, is. And perspective is the entire foundation upon which societies exist.

But in our time something strange has been at work upon our minds. The very generator of all life as we know it -- our Solar Eye in the sky -- has been throwing energy out more liberally than at any other time. I think it has been talking to the galactic center, and I think I know why. The very light that constitutes our atmosphere, our food intakes, our very bodies, has altered everything we are -- we have been upgraded by whom we know not. By "God" ultimately; but God is All of Us: there are Architects of reality we scarcely know how to contemplate -- and perhaps, just perhaps, on another scale of understanding entirely, those Architects are Us, our creator Primaries, orchestrating the dreams of possibilities and diving into them to be with us, *as* us, in the ups and downs of our ascendancies.

And so our national frameworks must come to an end. Like scaffolding, there is a time foreordained for their dis-mantling: a grander edifice stands within, that all our patriotisms, afterall, were aiming after. The groundswell of stewardship these past few decades has been noisily heralding, not only the rights of plants and animals, but the rights of even we human beings. Why, if a skunk is permitted a rent-free space in which to exist, with abundance of food and water, why not a man and a woman? Why is it that only the wild is free?

175

Why not the domesticated? If a tree-frog is allowed to have its forest, why not a tree-hugging child?

Stewardship, as a cultural phenomenon, gives an indication of something that has been in latency for generations, time out of mind; evidence that existential fear in human nature has not been the only motivator. The evolution of tribal villages into corporate cities, of nations into international neighborhoods, has not been solely driven by the herd instinct of self-preservation against invisible predators. *Love* has always been the glue that holds the warring parts together. Beneath our fears and institutions of self-protection, we congregate because we love each other, and want to give richly out of our private stores of innate wealth to lavish upon one another. Perceptions of poverty and impotence have only ever gotten in our way. The money culture has enacted a great deception before our eyes, but only because we were already addicted to the creature comforts of being slaves. We were still our brothers' keepers, even in our strongest chains, down in our deepest mines. Our wars were only someone else's; we went along for the ride. The sweat and blood of our fields, the arrogancy of our national prides, the double-humility of the daily grind and the mechanization of our lives -- even the sterilization of our minds -- always brought us back together after a short hiatus; a leg up over mutual defenses, a long leap over a length of trenches, even not speaking a single word of one another's goddamn language, and we were already tight with friends. We'd lay down our lives for each other now if we thought it would make our amends.

What I have called the Recolonization of Everything That's Already Been Started is a global phenomenon that is already well underway. It's something that starts deep underground in the ancient tunnels of the soul beneath a national fear and ignorance, and works its way upward to the surface of intelligence. It starts out a mystery and then becomes obvious. It's never in politics and finance that we find our answers. It's never in science, no matter how expensive the education. And since we're being honest, let us notice how religions do not really answer questions either; they are mostly there for consolation. Amidst all the circus noises of left and right opinions, the best answers always slip up from behind us with a whisper in quiet moments: in the unobtrusive symbols of our dreams; in seemingly random thoughts suggested out of unexpected sighs, curiously wise for afterthoughts neglected to the margins of our lives. We know more than we let on that we are knowing. Civilization, like anything else alive, starts from a sprout, grows from the inside out, and pushes inert stones aside in rushing after daylight. Last year's garden is nothing but leaves and twigs reduced to sod, returning nutrients to the soil for this year's up and coming generation of gods -- or call them a new breed of politicians in training, whose government is in their hearts. Today we are thinking in new paradigms. All the old familiarities are crumbling; we feel the tremor of them in the voice, like bidding a dying one good-bye. But these are necessary things, the way a burial also brings to mind the compliment of its relief, the setting aside of the dramas of change. Death and flowers have a way of stating things with that finality of power in occult signals. Strange, the way we can detect a kind of death in the cradle; and in the grave, the upthrust of everything new in the soil.

The colonies under formation today are not as easy to detect as bounded states. And it stands to reason, I guess. The old physically oriented way of demarcating jurisdictions need not be followed tomorrow, so there will not necessarily be regional and national counterparts -- no *territorial* designations -- carving up the social landscape of the next civilization, an octave higher, still a little out of our hearing range. Like a cyber network, a colony can be so "structured," so tentacled, as to encompass a given number of stewardships from widely diverse regions around the world, so that the multidimensionality of our minds achieves its mirroring in a multidimensional civilization, globally layered, many worlds in one. The "guilds," as I call them, may *tend* to unite in trade and cultural exchange and political representation due to their proximity; but with our technology able to link us up across boundary lines, national and international relations are at play *even at the guild level;* certainly at the broader colonial level as well.

But politics aside, the real promise of all this dreaming lies in the broadening of our minds, the setting aside of ancestral limitations, and the blossoming open of new sense spectrums. I have not talked extensively about the codicils which will make all this happen -- the guiding inclinations of our higher minds that amend our constitutions and bibles and other sacred parchments of that kind -- for it's not the words we use that alter the focus of our wills, it's the authenticity of our intentions. Codicils are best spoken than written; they are the natural expressions of a visionary mind intent upon self-renovation.

Governments, laws, and constitutions belong to the era of nations -- to the setting forth of forms and functions of government *under the rule of law*; those laws to be determined by that governing body so resolved upon. But now we are awash in a sea of laws, and they do not inspire confidence in their legitimacy; the lawmaking process itself is deeply compromised; and the very necessity for law, for external controls, only applies to people in their infancy -- to a people who have yet to master their own internal controls. Democracy, or self-government (collectively speaking), is no panacea, but a system of behaviors applicable for its time, till a greater maturity takes over -- till true self-government (individually speaking) arrives. Once *individuals* become truly self-governing, the laws and lawmaking democracies of their prior entrainment become increasingly unnecessary. The "rule of law" breaks down, not because of anarchy, but in *maturity*. Private, self-directed *will* takes over when an individual no longer needs the imposition of another's rule. He has discovered his own sovereignty. I suggest that this awakening is beginning to occur today.

Codicils are to sovereign individuals what a formal constitution is to citizens. It does not matter how they are written, or whether or not they are written down at all: they are only statements of intention rendered from an alternative world view than is characteristically mass marketed; a determination to live by different assumptions than those which have undermined every civilization so far of note. A steward repudiates the notion of vulnerability, and obeisance to critical authority -- whether a disapproving god or a meddling state. Truly, a civilization is built on human dignity, to say the least. The fall of civilizations can always be traced back to primal causes in the demoralization of individuals by their own beliefs. Dogmas of science and religion will poison us if we let them, and

178

become the basis of our governments and economies -- the predatory and oppressive state. But that is only if we let them, and "them" is *us*. By our own ingenuity we write riches into the ledgers our own inheritance; by our benightedness, we consign our innate prosperity to dust.

Prosperity is not what we are all looking for; it is what we are looking *from*. As stewards, our only task is to hold the vision for those who cannot comprehend this yet: that reality is not the morass of entangled beliefs to which we have succumbed. Reality is what we collapse it to be in the focal front of emotion. It is the mastery of environment through the mastering of ulterior motive, for environment is only intention made obvious.

It takes a certain daring to be legendary in a culture of pathos. But what do we care, having taken a giant leap away from our past cares. History has been but a long addiction. Tomorrow,... well... who knows?

It is up for self-prediction.

## ABOUT THE AUTHOR

**Troy Cochran** is a poet, philosopher, and essayist. He is the author of *The Gospel of Troy*, and *STONE & BONE: A Workingman's Poetry*, and numerous chapbooks. He maintains a blogsite at <u>trojanverses@blogsite.com</u>, and may be contacted via email at <u>delirioustill@gmail.com</u>. As a followup to *GENESIS*, he is currently writing on the themes of public stewardship, politics and economy in a book to be called *The Secret COMMONWEALTH*, to be followed by another on *The CODICILS.*

He resides with his daughter, Sarah, in the Pacific Northwest.